William Lindsay Alexander

St. Paul at Athens

William Lindsay Alexander

St. Paul at Athens

ISBN/EAN: 9783743317192

Manufactured in Europe, USA, Canada, Australia, Japa

Cover: Foto ©ninafisch / pixelio.de

Manufactured and distributed by brebook publishing software (www.brebook.com)

William Lindsay Alexander

St. Paul at Athens

BY

WILLIAM LINDSAY ALEXANDER, D.D.

EDINBURGH
ADAM AND CHARLES BLACK
1865

TO THE VERY REVEREND

E. B. RAMSAY, M.A., LL.D., F.R.S.E.

DEAN OF THE DIOCESE OF EDINBURGH,
ETC. ETC. ETC.

Dear Mr. Dean,

I gratify my own feelings of personal friendship in inscribing this little work to you. But I trust you will also accept it as a token of the respect with which your fellow-citizens of all religious denominations regard you, as one foremost in all works of Christian philanthropy, and who is an example to all of us how the most steadfast adherence to conviction may be combined with a generous appreciation of the character and motives of those who differ from us—reminding us that "faith unfeigned" has ever its fittest companion in that charity which "is kind," and "thinketh no evil."

With every sentiment of respect and esteem,

I am, dear Mr. Dean,

Most sincerely yours,

W. LINDSAY ALEXANDER.

PREFACE.

—ooo—

THIS volume contains the substance of a series of expository lectures, delivered by the author in the ordinary course of his ministry. The subjects handled by the apostle in his memorable address to the "Men of Athens," on Mars' Hill, are such as have engaged the attention of thoughtful men in all ages of the Church; and in the present day some of them have acquired special interest from the controversies of which they have been the theme. In expounding the apostle's address, it seemed to the author that a fitting occasion was furnished when, without mingling formally in these controversies, he might bring forward what appeared to him fitted to help inquirers to a just decision on the points at issue. He has, therefore, entered more at large into some of these subjects than mere exposition of the text required, especially the deeply-important subject of the Fatherhood of God. In respect of this he has sought to show that the position which Scripture authorises and teaches is a medium position between the opinion of those who would restrict God's Fatherhood to his gracious special relation to redeemed men, and that of those who deny any such special relation, and maintain that God is not a Father to any in a sense in which He is not a Father to all.

To facilitate the understanding of the topographical references in the earlier lectures, the following plan of ancient Athens may be found useful.

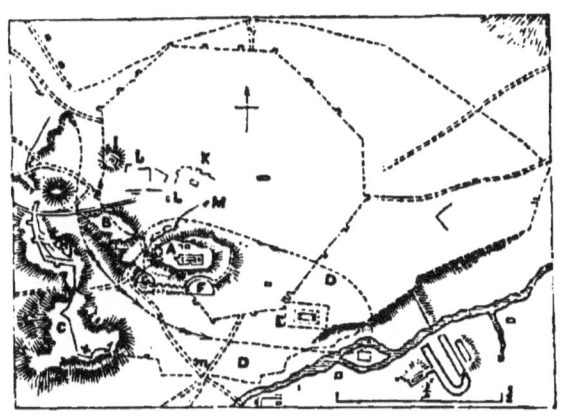

A. The Acropolis.
B. Areopagus.
C. Museium.
D. Hadrianopolis.
E. Temple of Jupiter Olympius.
F. Theatre of Bacchus.
G. Odeium of Regilla.
H. Pnyx.
I. Temple of Theseus.
J. Gymnasium of Ptolemy.
K. Stoa of Hadrian.
L. Gate of New Agora.
M. Tower of Andronicus.

CONTENTS.

—ooo—

		PAGE
I.	St. Paul in the Agora	3
II.	St. Paul on Mars' Hill	31
III.	St. Paul's Discourse—God and the Universe	60
IV.	St. Paul's Discourse—the Fatherhood of God	87
V.	St. Paul's Discourse—Unity of the Human Race	111
VI.	St. Paul's Discourse—Consequences Flowing out of the Divine Fatherhood to the Race	144
VII.	Erroneous Representations of the Fatherhood of God	170
VIII.	St. Paul's Discourse—God a King and Judge as well as Father	199
IX.	St. Paul's Discourse.—God's Summons of all Men to Repent—the Final Judgment .	226
X.	St. Paul's Discourse—Conclusion and Result	266
XI.	St. Paul's Abiding Confidence in Christianity as the Power of God and the Wisdom of God	291

ST. PAUL AT ATHENS.

—ooo—

ACTS xvii. 16-34.

Now, while Paul waited for them at Athens, his spirit was stirred in him, when he saw the city wholly given to idolatry. Therefore disputed he in the synagogue with the Jews, and with the devout persons, and in the market daily with them that met with him.

Then certain philosophers of the Epicureans, and of the Stoicks, encountered him. And some said, What will this babbler say? other some, He seemeth to be a setter forth of strange gods: because he preached unto them Jesus, and the resurrection. And they took him, and brought him unto Areopagus, saying, May we know what this new doctrine, whereof thou speakest, is? For thou bringest certain strange things to our ears: we would know therefore what these things mean. (For all the Athenians, and strangers which were there, spent their time in nothing else, but either to tell, or to hear some new thing.)

Then Paul stood in the midst of Mars' hill, and said, Ye men of Athens, I perceive that in all things ye are too superstitious. For as I passed by, and beheld your devotions, I found an altar with this inscription, To THE UNKNOWN GOD. Whom therefore ye ignorantly worship,

Him declare I unto you. God, that made the world, and all things therein, seeing that He is Lord of heaven and earth, dwelleth not in temples made with hands; neither is worshipped with men's hands, as though He needed anything, seeing He giveth to all life, and breath, and all things; and hath made of one blood all nations of men for to dwell on all the face of the earth, and hath determined the times before appointed, and the bounds of their habitation; that they should seek the LORD, if haply they might feel after Him, and find Him, though he be not far from every one of us: for in Him we live, and move, and have our being; as certain also of your own poets have said, *For we are also His offspring.* Forasmuch then as we are the offspring of God, we ought not to think that the Godhead is like unto gold, or silver, or stone, graven by art and man's device. And the times of this ignorance God winked at; but now commandeth all men everywhere to repent: because He hath appointed a day, in the which He will judge the world in righteousness by that man whom He hath ordained; whereof He hath given assurance unto all men, in that He hath raised Him from the dead.

And when they heard of the resurrection of the dead, some mocked: and others said, We will hear thee again of this matter.

So Paul departed from among them. Howbeit certain men clave unto him, and believed: among the which was Dionysius the Areopagite, and a woman named Damaris, and others with them.

I.

St. Paul in the Agora.

The visit of the Apostle Paul to Athens was made not long after his first landing on the shores of Europe. Having preached the gospel with success at Philippi, Thessalonica, and Berea, he was compelled to leave his companions, Silas and Timothy, at the last of these places, and escape by sea from the persevering malice of the Jews, who had followed him from Thessalonica. Athens having been appointed as the place of reunion with his companions, the apostle abode there waiting their arrival; and during this visit occurred the circumstances narrated in the passage which I propose to make the subject of exposition and illustration.

In what manner the apostle occupied his

time during the earlier period of his visit, we are not informed, but from what is stated, both by the historian and by himself, as to the extent of survey which he bestowed upon the ways of the inhabitants, we may presume that he spent some time in contemplating the objects of interest which the famous city to which he had been conducted supplied.[1] There was no city in the ancient world that had within its precincts so much to attract the attention and excite the admiration of the man of taste and culture, as Athens. Nobly situated, and filled with the most exquisite works in architecture and sculpture which the genius of the most aesthetic people in the world could supply; surrounded by an atmosphere so transparent

---

[1] Luke uses the participle ἐκδεχόμενος in reference to the apostle's abode in Athens, and the verb θεωρεῖν to describe the careful and thorough inspection which he gave to its religious phenomena. Paul himself uses still stronger terms (ver. 23), διερχόμενος καὶ ἀναθεωρῶν τὰ σεβάσματα ὑμῶν. This implies that he went *through* the city, and minutely surveyed their religious things. (Compare Heb. xiii. 7, for the force of ἀναθεωρεῖν).

and genial that the most delicately-finished works of art could be placed without injury in the open air, and the inhabitants could live and worship, and legislate, and teach, and debate under the canopy of heaven;[1] while over all looked in unclouded splendour the "unresting eye of day,"[2] bathing in golden or purple light rock and stream, fluted column and massive temple; Athens stood forth the glory of the "bright land"[3] of which it was the metropolis, the pride of Greece and the wonder of the world. To the attraction of such a scene we cannot suppose that the mind of the apostle was insensible; perhaps there might be in it for him a deep charm to which it would be a joy for him to yield his soul. But he was not in circumstances to resign himself to such fascinations. There are higher objects of con-

---

[1] ἀεὶ διὰ λαμπροτάτου βαίνοντες ἀβρῶς αἰθέρος. Eurip. *Med.* 825.

[2] ὄμμα αἰθέρος ἀκάματον σελαγεῖται.— Aristoph *Clouds*, 285.

[3] λιπαρὰν χθόνα.—*Ibid.* 299.

templation than those which gratify the taste; and the mind may be so absorbed in great themes of intellectual or moral interest as to be well nigh insensible to all the charms of scenery, and all the attractions of art. When Howard went forth, on what a great orator has called his " circumnavigation of charity," he visited some of the noblest cities, and passed through some of the most attractive scenery of modern Europe; but neither the splendour and wealth of the one, nor the attractions of the other, could engage his attention; the dungeon and the hospital, where suffering humanity invited his aid, had an interest to his mind which drew him aside from everything else, and made him insensible " to the sumptousness of palaces and the stateliness of temples," to the curiosity of art, and even to the sublimities and beauties of nature. Cicero tells us, that for him Athens had a higher charm than was derived from its magnificent buildings and exquisite works of art,—the charm that arose from the memory of its illustrious men, and which made him search out the abodes and favourite haunts of each, and look with intent gaze on their sepulchres.[1] In all large and earnest minds the moral will ever overtop and master the aesthetic; and, save as the latter may in some way be made subservient to the former, such minds will be apt to overlook, if not entirely to underestimate it. What wonder, then, that Paul, bent on a mission of moral beneficence to which he had consecrated his life, and penetrated with an all-absorbing desire to accomplish a result which he knew to be the noblest and worthiest and most enduring that could be proposed to human exertion, should have been content to bestow only a passing glance on the marble splendours of Athens, and should have been more deeply moved by the gloom which rested on the moral features of the scene, than by all the glory which lighted up its physical and material aspect? As he moved through the city, he beheld how all this wealth of genius

[1] De Legibus, ii. 1.

was prostituted to the service of a vain and misleading superstition; how all this surpassing beauty which, as it was fabled, had made the city of the purple crown an object of contention even to immortals themselves,[1] had but served as a veil to hide from men's minds the knowledge of Him of whose glory it was the reflection and the witness; and how men, surrounded by all that was fitted to refine and spiritualise and elevate the mind, were nevertheless grovelling under the degrading influence of a grossly sensuous and debasing idolatry. Paul was not the man to behold such a scene unmoved. Accustomed to look at things in their spiritual, rather than in their material aspects, he took in the whole picture of moral defilement and misery which lay under this smiling and gorgeous exterior. At the sight his soul was stirred within him, and with fearless zeal, yet with a tact and sagacity which bespoke him no vain enthusiast, he cast himself into the busy, noisy

[1] Herod. viii. 55; Pausan. i. 24. 5.

A CITY FULL OF IDOLS.

stream of Athenian life, if haply he might, in some measure at least, arrest its downward course, and turn it in the direction where alone light and blessedness could be found.

St. Paul saw the city "wholly given to idolatry." The original rather means he saw the city full of idols;[1] and this description is one which is amply borne out by the statements of the classical writers, who speak of the Athenians as exceeding all others in zeal for sacred rites, and describe Athens as "containing altars and temples in every direction;" as full of "statues of gods and men, of every kind and material, and in every variety of art;" and as one vast altar, sacrifice and offering.[2] Wandering amid such objects, beholding in every street and on every prominent point some symbol or instrument of idolatrous worship, unable to enjoy the beauty of God's earth, because

---

[1] κατείδωλον οὖσαν τὴν πόλιν.

[2] See the passages collected by Wetstein in his note on Acts xvii. 16, *Nov. Test. Gr.* ii. p. 562.

everywhere his eye lighted on some elaborate work of man that was an insult to the majesty, and a virtual denial of the existence of the One Living and True God; it is not wonderful that the apostle's righteous soul should have been vexed, and his spirit stirred within him. Not, however, with scorn or indignation was he chiefly moved. Such feelings the sight of a city full of objects of idolatrous worship might move in the bosom of an enlightened theist, for under certain of its aspects, idolatry is so contemptible, so foolish, so God-dishonouring and man-degrading, that it is difficult to think of it without some emotions of contempt or wrath towards those who follow it. But in the mind of the apostle such feelings, we may be well assured, would be speedily absorbed in one deep and overwhelming emotion of pity for those who were suffering themselves to be ensnared, and fettered, and blinded to their eternal ruin, by such delusions. In every statue and temple and altar he would see but an additional instrument for the destruction of immortal souls. The very wealth of art, that poured itself out before him, would be to him but the measure of the spiritual poverty, humiliation, and wretchedness of the people. He knew that idolatry always brings moral degradation and misery in its train, even where intellectual culture and artistic skill may have thrown an air of glory over the worship, and an aspect of refinement over the surface of society. To his enlightened vision, the splendid and beautiful Athens was but like one of her own marble sepulchres —outwardly fair and attractive, but " within full of dead men's bones and all uncleanness."

And so a necessity came upon him to get to work and proclaim the gospel to these idolaters. Whether he had come to Athens with this intention we are not told; though from his known zeal and activity, we can well believe that from the time of his approach to the city this would be what he was anxious to do. But it is not surprising that before adventuring on so new and difficult an enterprise, he should have desired the presence and support of his friends, whom he had left behind at Berea. In prospect of this, his first purpose had been to delay operations until their arrival. But the sight of this exuberant and rampant idolatry so wrought upon him, that it became impossible for him to carry out that intention. All considerations of personal comfort and advantage gave way before the stirrings of holy zeal and compassionate pity which the scene provoked. And so, unhesitatingly he threw himself into the arena, and stood up to do battle, single-handed and alone, for God and for truth, against the wit, wisdom, science, and dialectic skill of the most refined, ingenious, and cultivated people of the world.

True to his national predilections, which never suffered him to neglect his brethren according to the flesh, he addressed himself in the first instance to the Jews and proselytes[1] whom he found in Athens, visiting for

---

[1] "Devout persons" (τοῖς σεβομένοις), phraseology used to denote those who, born heathens, had been turned from idols to fear and worship the true God.

this purpose their synagogue, and holding conversations with them.¹ Thus far he acted as he had always done since he became an apostle of Christ; but it was not long until he ventured upon a hitherto untried course. Near to the centre of the city was a large open space called the Agora, where were several of the public buildings of Athens, and which was full of monuments of religious and patriotic interest to the Athenians. Here at all times were to be found multitudes of people drawn together by the calls of business, or by the Athenian love of talk; and here any one who wished to inculcate any doctrines, speculative or practical, was sure to find, if not an attentive audience, at least abundance of acute and eager logicians, ready to discuss with him any subject, human or divine, on which he chose to

---

¹ The word used, διελέγετο, means literally that a dialogue took place between him and them. The character of this would often doubtless be controversial; but the word does not necessarily mean, as our version gives it, "disputed."

speak. Through this place the apostle had doubtless occasion frequently to pass, and as he did so he took the opportunity of drawing some of the many idlers around him into conversation. This was a new sphere for the apostle, whose labours had hitherto been confined to synagogues and private companies; but being once embarked in it, he gave himself to it with all his native energy and heroism, so that it at length became his "daily" practice. His custom seems to have been to get into talk with any whom he chanced to meet.[1] He did not ostentatiously throw down the gauntlet to the chiefs of the great philosophic schools which then divided the allegiance of the speculatists of Greece but was content to speak with any one who was willing to hear what he had to say. It was not long, however, before he came in contact with the philosophers, abundance of whom might be at all times found in the Agora. The historian mentions two sects, the disciples of which he encountered in debate,—

[1] παρατυγχάνοντας.

the Stoics and the Epicureans. Of all the sects of Grecian philosophy, these were the two most likely to come into collision with one engaged in such a work as that to which St. Paul was devoted. Of the other sects, some had renounced the search after truth as hopeless, and had abandoned themselves to absolute scepticism; while others indulged in etherial speculations belonging to a purely ideal region, and having little relation to actual life or the concrete interests of mankind. For neither of these classes had the busy pragmatical Agora much attraction; and from such questions as Paul was likely to bring forward,—questions relating to man's duties, obligations, and prospects, and the solution of which was offered, not as the reward of philosophic inquiry, but through the medium of an objective revelation,—these sceptical or sublime speculatists were likely to turn aside at once with contempt or indifference. With the Stoics and the Epicureans it was different. The aim of both was practical rather than speculative. They sought to settle the foundations of virtue, and to give men directions how to conduct themselves, so as to make the best of life's experiences. According to the former, virtue consisted in living according to nature, and the wise man was he who regulated his daily life so as to keep himself in harmony with the great ends and purposes of his being, not allowing himself to be elated with prosperity, as if that were a good in itself, or to be overwhelmed with adversity, as if that were an evil in itself. To this the doctrine of the Epicureans was to a great extent antithetical. They taught that the main end of man's life and being was happiness, and therefore they counselled men, on the one hand, to avoid all sources of discomfort or suffering, and, among the rest, foolish and wicked conduct, which was sure to bring suffering, if not directly, yet by a retributive remorse; and on the other, to cultivate whatever has a tendency to soothe the soul, and make life flow on softly and sweetly. Both schools thus professed to tell men how to be good and blessed; both, therefore, naturally sought disciples among the masses; and both came thus, as well by the nature of their doctrines as by the area of their activity, into collision with the apostle as a teacher of Christianity. For he, too, came to tell men how they might be wise, and good, and blessed; and as he claimed for his doctrine a preference to all that philosophy had to teach on these points, it was inevitable that, as he taught in the Agora at Athens, he should have to abide the encounter of the adherents of these schools.

The result of these discussions was remarkable. When one considers that Paul was a foreigner, who, even if he spoke Greek idiomatically, would speak it with an accent that could not but offend ears so delicate as those of the Athenians, among whom even the market women could not refrain from correcting the mispronunciation of their foreign customers; and when, further, it is borne in mind that much of what he had to say would of necessity be new and strange to his auditors, it cannot appear surprising that some should have turned scornfully aside with the question, "What will this babbler say?" that is, What does he want to say? What would he be at?[1] and that others, attracted by the novelty of his doctrines—impressed perhaps by the manifest sincerity and earnestness of the man, yet utterly at sea as to the purport of his teaching—should have exclaimed, "He seemeth to be a setter forth of strange gods."

This latter exclamation, Luke tells us, was provoked especially by Paul's preaching to them Jesus and the Resurrection. From the use of the plural, "gods," some have been led to suppose that the Athenians took Jesus for one, and Anastasis, or the Resur-

[1] The original conveys this: τί ἄν θέλοι σπερμολόγος δυτος λέγειν; what may he be wishing to say? The epithet σπερμολόγος, *grain-gatherer*, was originally applied to the rook; and as used of men, conveyed the notion sometimes of a person who picks up scraps of knowledge from others, sometimes of one loquacious, garrulous, and empty. "*Babbler* is the very best English word, as best signifying one who talks fluently to no purpose, and hinting also that his talk is *not his own*."—Alford, on the passage.

rection, for another of the deities, whose worship Paul was seeking to introduce into Athens, famed for its hospitality as well to foreign gods as men.[1] But though it is probable that the doctrine of the Resurrection was new and strange to these philosophers, we can hardly suppose that the apostle would have expressed himself so strangely as to lead them to imagine that, in speaking of it, he was speaking of a person, or would have them place it on a footing with Jesus. Doubtless what Paul preached on this occasion, was the divine claim of Jesus to be regarded as the Son of God and the Saviour of the world—a claim of which His resurrection from the dead was the crowning attestation and proof. On this great fact Paul was wont to lay peculiar stress in his preaching, partly because of the authority which it imparted to his doctrine, partly because it

---

[1] "The Athenians are hospitable as in other respects, so also in respect of the gods. For they have received many foreign religions, for which they were ridiculed in the comedies." Strabo, *Geogr.* x. p. 471.

formed the security of that great privilege which he was commissioned to offer to men —the pardon of sin through the merit of the Saviour's intercession, and the prospect of eternal felicity with Him in a future state. Of such things philosophy had not dreamt, and therefore when Paul connected this in his preaching with the claims of Jesus, these acute Athenians saw at once that he asserted for Jesus divine honour, and so represented him as "a setter forth of strange gods." The use of the plural may be accounted for on grammatical grounds;[1] or, perhaps, as Paul could hardly preach Jesus and the Resurrection without a reference to God the Father, some confusion and misapprehension might lead these philosophers to suppose that he was advocating the claims of *two* new deities.

What is thus ascribed to Paul formed one of the main charges brought against Socrates, and on which that most illustrious of the sons of Athens was condemned to

[1] See Kuinœl on the passage.

death.[1] But whilst it might be criminal for a citizen to seem to despise his country's gods by introducing those of another people, it does not appear that it was so for a foreigner to set forth the claims of his own deities. In this respect a certain liberty seems to have been allowed at Athens, and a place was even conceded to foreign deities beside those that were indigenous. It was not, therefore, as charged with a crime that Paul was carried to the Areopagus, where the supreme court of Athens had its seat, but merely that a more commodious place might be obtained for him in which to expound his novel message. It was curiosity, not anger, which moved to this step. His hearers wished to know fully, and without the interruptions which in the Agora were inevitable, what this doctrine of his was.

The apostle on Mars' Hill we leave for subsequent contemplation. In the meantime there are one or two considerations of a

---

[1] Xenophon, *Memorabilia*, I. 1., 1.

general kind, arising out of the verses we have been studying, to which it may be well briefly to advert.

1. We see here Christianity, in the person of one of its most eminent teachers, brought into contact with art in its higher forms. Now, it must certainly " be admitted," as has been remarked,[1] " to be highly significant and important, that the first impressions which the master-pieces of man's taste for art left on the mind of St. Paul was a revolting one." But whence did this revulsion of feeling arise? Not surely from any conviction in the mind of the apostle that art was in itself an unlawful pursuit, or that it might not be worthily connected with religion; for, as a Jew, accustomed to the temple and its services at Jerusalem, no such conviction could have found place in his mind. Was there, then, anything in Christianity, as a religious system, hostile to art, either in itself, or in its application to reli-

---

[1] Lechler on the place in Lange's *Bibelwerk*, pt. 5.

gious uses? This can hardly be affirmed in the face of the fact, that Christianity has everywhere, not only shown an affinity with art, but has, more than any other influence, dignified and glorified it. No; as the writer already cited justly adds: It was because " all this majesty and beauty had placed itself between man and his Creator, and bound him the faster to his gods, which were not God," that painful feelings were roused in the bosom of the apostle. The emotions of delight, which the art itself might have excited, were prevented by the feelings of mingled indignation and pity with which the sight of the grievous abuse of it, prostituted as it was to the service of idolatry, filled his soul.

Artistic power is as truly a divine gift as intellect and moral feeling, and in its own place has an important bearing on the catholic development of man's inner nature, and may be made, in a high degree, subservient to his religious culture. But, like all God's gifts to us, it may be abused; and just because of its greater delicacy and finer temper the abuse of it may result in something viler and more degrading than it is possible for other parts of our nature to furnish. The abuses to which it is liable are especially two. The one is, when it becomes an all-absorbing passion, exercising an imperious tyranny over the soul, making all things bend to its gratification, measuring the good or evil of things simply by their power to minister to its cravings, and tempting him who is the subject of it to trifle with the most sacred obligations, and postpone the most important duties, in obedience to its demands. The other is, when it lends itself to unholy, profane, impure, or unworthy uses; when it is employed to confirm man in his ungodliness; when it becomes the minister of superstition or sacerdotal craft; or when it throws its enchantment around what is degrading, and paints a beautiful mask for the foul and ghastly face of vice. In all such cases, art assumes a position which compels the moralist and the man of spiritual religion to bear towards it a hostile front, and denounce it as evil and dangerous.

2. Christianity appears here also, in the person of the apostle, for the first time in contact with human systems of philosophic speculation. And here the same is to be said, in substance, that has been already said in relation to art. To philosophy, as such, Christianity cannot be hostile. The great questions of which she offers the solution are precisely those with which philosophy, in its higher forms, is occupied; and there is no better preparation for the lessons she has to teach, and no surer voucher for their sufficiency, in relation to the mind's wants and capacities, than philosophy, wisely and legitimately exercised, is fitted to furnish. It is not surprising, therefore, that from the earliest ages Christianity has found in philosophy her readiest and deftest handmaid. But, from the earliest ages also, philosophy has been the antagonist and the perverter of Christianity. The writings of St. Paul indicate a mind naturally inclined to philosophic research, and

disciplined by the methods and lessons of philosophy; but St. Paul had occasion to caution the Christians to whom he wrote against a "philosophy," which is only "an empty cheat," and "oppositions of science falsely so called."[1] It is to the application of philosophic principles and methods, by such men as Augustine, Anselm, Aquinas, and Calvin, that the church is indebted for the full and scientific development of that doctrinal system, the elements of which are scattered through the pages of Holy Scripture; but it is no less to the mingling of philosophic speculations with the teachings of Scripture, that the Church owes most of those heretical opinions by which her testimony has been corrupted and her peace disturbed, from the time of Simon Magus downwards. There is a necessity, therefore, for caution and discrimination on the part of the followers of Christ when they are brought into contact with the schools of human philosophy, that they may wisely choose the good and refuse the evil

[1] Col. ii. 8 ; 1 Tim. vi. 20.

among the doctrines which these schools profess. Holding fast "the truth as it is in Jesus," repudiating all attempts to modify or supplement the divine word by the conclusions of human wisdom, and not shrinking from boldly encountering the disciples of any school of philosophy when they cross their path, let them at the same time willingly accept whatever aids philosophy may be prepared to render as the handmaid of theology, either in illustration or in defence of the truths most surely believed amongst them.

3. As some of those philosophers whom Paul encountered in the Agora of Athens heard his doctrines only to turn from them and him with contempt, so there are still men who, professing to be students of philosophy and searchers after truth, think it not incompatible with these pretensions to treat Christianity with similar light-minded rejection. Many, indeed, do this from mere indifference to all religious interests; but others, professing to recognise religion as the

supreme concern of man, hastily repudiate Christianity on the ground of some foregone conclusion at which they have arrived. To one man a revelation of religious truth from without appears unnecessary and incongruous, the spiritual nature of man being held by him to be sufficient for the evolution of a religion for itself; by another, a book-revelation is regarded as an absurdity, and the very idea of submission to it scouted as an insult to man's intellectual supremacy; while a third, having settled in his own mind that a miracle is impossible, regards the fact that Christianity is a miraculous religion as sufficient to justify him in passing it by with neglect. Such methods of dealing with such a subject are, to say the least, unphilosophical as well as unwise. The first lesson which true science teaches is, to regard all things possible which are not self-contradictory, and to reject, on purely *a priori* grounds, nothing that claims to rest on a basis of fact. He who believes in God will not lightly pronounce it impossible or improbable that the Creator should communicate directly the knowledge of His will to His intelligent and accountable creatures; and to every serious and earnest thinker it must ever appear that the mere possibility of a given book containing a message from God imposes on all to whom it comes an obligation to examine, with all candour and earnestness, the evidence on which it rests its claims. This much Christianity, as a professed revelation from God, has a right to demand, and whilst every honest searcher after truth will concede this right, and submit to it, the risks of neglecting to do this are so tremendous that no wise man will lightly incur them. Christianity asks no one to listen to her teaching until he has satisfied himself of the truth of her claims; but to refuse so much as to look at these claims on the ground of some foregone conclusion, her advocates cannot but denounce as alike arrogant and foolish. Strange that men who are forward to proclaim that it is only by acting as "the minister and interpreter of nature" that any one can hope to arrive at natural truth, should imagine that divine truth may be reached by a simple process of *a priori* deduction and subjective preference!

II.

St. Paul on Mars' Hill.

ATHENS embraced within its precints several natural elevations. One of these was the Areopagus or Mars' Hill; so called, according to popular tradition, because Ares or Mars had been brought to trial there before the assembled gods for the murder of Halirrhothius, the son of Poseidon. It is described as "a narrow, naked ridge of limestone rock, rising gradually from the northern end, and terminating abruptly on the south;" reaching on this end a height of between fifty and sixty feet above the level of the valley at its base. It stands very near to the Agora, in which the apostle commenced his discussions with the Athenians; and the steps still remain, cut in the rock, by which it was ascended on that side. On the summit of the rock, just above the Agora, was the spot where the judges of the Upper Council sat and administered justice in the open air; their seat was a stone bench cut in the rock, which still remains. It was not (as already observed), however, as a criminal that St. Paul was conveyed to this spot, nor was the manner of the act indicative of any disrespect to him on the part of those who had surrounded him in the Agora. On the contrary, the expression used by Luke, and rendered in our version, "they took him" (ver. 19), conveys in the original the idea of gentle and courteous handling;[1] and the historian is careful to tell us that it was curiosity and not displeasure which prompted the removal to the Areopagus. With the Athenians this was a motive which had all the power of a ruling passion. Luke says of them here, that "all the Athenians and strangers which were there spent their time in nothing else but either to tell or to hear some new thing"

---

[1] ἐπιλαβόμενοι, "manu leniter prehensum" Grotius, *in loc.*

(ver. 21). The statement here is somewhat stronger in the translation than in the original, which simply indicates that they had leisure for nothing else;[1] that their whole spare time was spent in hearing and telling the latest news.[2] But even thus modified, the statement is so sweeping that one might be tempted to set it down, in part at least, to the prejudice of a foreigner, accustomed to the stiller life and graver manners of the east, and to whom, therefore, the busy, bustling, inquisitive, talkative habits of the Athenians could not but be annoying, were it not that Athenian testimonies themselves amply establish the charge. Indeed, Demosthenes, in one of his addresses to his countrymen, reproaches them with this propensity in language almost identical with that of Luke,[3]

---

[1] εὐκαιρεῖν, a later word not used by the best Greek writers, who employed σχολαζειν in the same sense, that of being at leisure.

[2] καινότερον, literally a newer thing, *i. e.*, something newer than what was last new, the latest news.

[3] *Philip.* i. 5, Comp. Thucyd. iii. 38 ; Aelian, *Hist. Var.* v. 13 ; Seneca, *Ep.* 94, etc.

and other witnesses abundantly attest the same thing. To such persons anything really new was a perfect treasure, which they could not too eagerly appropriate; and therefore, recognising in what Paul said to them something they had never heard before, they carried him to the Areopagus that they might have space and quiet to hear what he had to tell. But amidst this giddy crowd, who hastened up the steps of the Areopagus as they might have hurried to a comedy, may we not suppose there were some influenced by better feelings than those of mere curiosity—some who recognised in what St. Paul had already uttered, something more than mere novel talk—some who, really seeking for truth, had found a strange response in their inner nature to what had fallen from his lips—some who, in the foreign and strange doctrines which he announced, saw, as by the glimmer of a distant lamp, a possible pathway out of the maze of speculation in which they were lost; and who, therefore, spoke in honest earnestness when they said, "We wish to know what these things mean." At any rate, their language to the apostle was perfectly courteous. What they asked, they asked as a favour: "May we know what this new doctrine whereof thou speakest [this new teaching of which thou art the expounder] is?"

To such a request the apostle could have no unwillingness to accede. Some little natural agitation and anxiety might probably, for the moment, take hold of him as he anticipated a scene so novel and so trying as that in which he was about to be the principal actor. But this would soon pass away, absorbed in the nobler emotions which the prospect of proclaiming the truth, of which he was the herald, on so conspicuous a platform and to so interesting an audience, would awaken in his soul; or if this could not wholly disperse these feelings, all tendency to shrink from the ordeal through which he had to pass would be rebuked as he remembered the assurance of his Divine Master,

"When they shall lead you and deliver you up, take no thought beforehand what you shall speak, neither premeditate; but whatsoever shall be given you in that hour, that speak ye; for it is not ye that speak but the Holy Ghost."[1]

And now the apostle has ascended the steps, and stands on the summit of the Areopagus. What a scene presents itself to his view! Close beside him is the crowd of citizens who have followed him from the Agora, and intermingled with them are not only the philosophers who have chiefly provoked this scene, but also some of the principal persons of the city, and one at least of the judges of the Areopagus. Before and around him lies the city in all its natural beauty, and in all its wealth of art. A little to the east of where he stands rises the Acropolis, abrupt and vast, covered with the noblest monuments of Grecian art—temples, and theatres, and statues, and sculptured groups—rising up in simple but majestic beauty from the stately

[1] Matt. xiii. 11.

Propylæea to the sublime Parthenon, the masterpiece and the glory of ancient architecture. On the other side, also close by the Agora, rises the Pnyx, the place of the assemblies of the people, where stands the famous stone from which the orators addressed the assembled multitude, and from which had often sounded the voice of him

> " whose resistless eloquence
> Wielded at will that fierce democracy,
> Shook the arsenal, and fulmined over Greece
> To Macedon and Artaxerxes' throne."

In other directions, other spots famous in history or sacred to literature and philosophy, as well as beautified by art, meet the eye, and solicit attention. But Paul is not there to feast his imagination, or sate his taste with this opulence of artistic splendour. He has come thither, filled with the inspiration of a message from God, to tell these polished idolaters of the perfections and the claims of that one only God, of whom they had well-nigh utterly lost sight amid the multitude and variety of their mythological inventions; and full of this, he has no eyes for either the charms of nature or the glories of art; or if the scene before him for a moment attracts his attention, the sight of so much genius prostituted to the worst of uses, only kindles his zeal to greater fervour, and gives him fresh courage to assail the adversary in this the very palace of his glory and citadel of his strength. And so the apostle stands up, undaunted though alone, in the midst of that polished auditory to lift up his testimony for God and for truth, in opposition to their most cherished prejudices and their most favoured beliefs.

With whatever other feelings the multitude around him might regard the apostle, it would be impossible for them not to respect and admire the courage of the man. Never did orator stand up to address an audience under greater disadvantages. Everything almost of an outward kind was against him. His being a foreigner was against him; for the Athenians, who boasted that they had sprung from the soil of Attica, looked upon all other nations with contempt, and spoke of them as barbarians. His speech was against him; for, to the fine ears of the Athenians, accustomed to hear their exquisite language uttered with the nicest attention to pronunciation and accent, it must have been well-nigh intolerable to hear it spoken by one whose speech was, by his own confession, contemptible, even in the esteem of the less fastidious Corinthians.[1] His personal appearance was against him; for he was of diminutive stature, and his bodily presence was feeble, whilst around him were the graceful forms and noble countenances of the most perfectly-developed race that the world has ever seen. His subject was against him; for he stood there to denounce the religious beliefs and usages of the Hellenic nations in the very centre of the Hellenic worship, and in the midst of a people enthusiastically devoted to their national superstitions; to assail the time-honoured prejudices of the haughtiest and most self-confident of peoples;

[1] 2 Cor. x. 10.

and in a city full of idols, and swarming with philosophers, to prove idolatry a wicked absurdity, and philosophy, such as they had it, a delusion and a snare. It was, indeed, a bold thing for such a man to venture on such an attempt under such circumstances; and one can fancy that, as the speaker raised his unimposing form, and stretched forth his feeble arm, when about to commence his address, any feelings of surprise or contempt which his appearance at first might excite, would speedily give place to those of respect and admiration, such as true bravery never fails to evoke.

Trying as was the task to which he was summoned, the apostle was fully equal to it. And, in truth, amidst the outward disadvantages to which I have alluded, he possessed qualities of another kind which more than turned the balance in his favour. For one thing, his mind as much overtopped the minds of the mass of his audience as their physical endowments excelled his. His was really the freest and kingliest spirit of the whole.

Not that in respect of mere original power of intellect he surpassed all who then surrounded him, for on this point we have no means of forming an opinion; but that there was no mind there that could so thoroughly grasp and comprehend him as his mind could grasp and comprehend them. Insignificant as he seemed in respect of outward appearance, he could take the measure and weight of the whole assembly as they could not do of him. None of them had so largely and so truly surveyed humanity in all its interests, relations, and wants as he had; nor could any so minister to the deepest necessities of the human heart as he could. Much as some of those beside him had speculated on things divine, he alone had seen God as He reveals Himself to His people; and he alone could speak of divine things with the firmness and assurance of one who speaks because he believes. In short, he had the power which truth and knowledge confer; and he needed but this opportunity of free speech to vindicate for himself the influence and authority which the possessor of these always gains over those who are the slaves of error or of ignorance.

The oration which the apostle delivered on this occasion has called forth the admiration of the most competent judges of all subsequent ages and countries. It is marked not only by a calm dignity and thorough mastery of the topics discussed, but by a wonderful adaptation to the peculiar condition and mental habits of those to whom he spoke, and by a constructive ability altogether marvellous in a discourse composed on the spur of the moment, and by one who had enjoyed no previous training or experience in rhetoric. Viewed simply in itself, we may well call it a masterpiece of the highest style of oratory; skilfully adapted to the audience, and yet severely faithful to truth; fitted to persuade, by convincing the judgment without alarming prejudice or offending taste; calculated to stimulate and guide all the higher powers of man, so as to bring the hearer of his own accord, and with the full assent of his will, to the conclusion the speaker would enforce.

Viewed in relation to himself, the whole address remarkably exhibits the tact and power of the man, and strikingly illustrates his own declaration that he became "all things to all men;" that to the Jews he was as a Jew, and to the Greeks he was as a Greek, not for the sake of securing honour, favour, or applause, but in the sublime hope of thereby saving some.[1] And herein, we may remark in passing, lay one great secret of his power. His soul was *set* on the great end of his mission; in the pursuit of this all considerations of a minor kind were lost; and he adjusted himself to the case he had in hand with the ease and naturalness of one who seeks not his own things, but the good of those whom he addresses. In this outgoing of the individual upon his object lies the secret of all great success in public address. If a man is more concerned to do justice to himself or to his subject than to

[1] 1 Cor. ix. 20-22.

win those to whom he speaks; or if he be more anxious to keep himself in accordance with the dogmas of some school, or the articles of some church, than to get into a living sympathy with the souls and hearts of those whom he addresses, he will certainly fail of being a great orator, whatever excellence in other respects he may attain. In the pulpit such an one may prove himself a luminous expositor, an acute polemic, an exact reasoner, a profound theologian, but he will never attain the reputation of an eloquent or greatly successful preacher. It was the apostle's peculiar gift that he could combine all these excellences, and whether as the expositor, the theologian, the polemic, or the preacher, assert for himself a foremost place, and subject other men to his imperial sway. Let us never forget that he owed this not to mere natural endowment, but to the presence and constant aid of the Spirit of his Master. This he would himself have been forward to proclaim, and it is for us who admire his gifts, and profit by what he accomplished through the use of them, humbly to acknowledge the grace of God in him, and to glorify God on his behalf.

The apostle commences his speech to the Athenians exactly as one of their own orators might have done; indeed, he addresses them in the very words which are so familiar to the readers of the classics, as those by which Demosthenes always addressed his countrymen—words the very sound of which sent a thrill through the heart of every Athenian.[1] "Men of Athens"—*men* in the higher sense of the term, not mere human beings, but men worthy of the name—"Men of Athens," exclaims the apostle, "I perceive that in every way ye are very religious," or, as the word should perhaps be rendered, strictly according to its form, "*more* religious," that is than the rest of your countrymen.[2] The translation in the Authorised Version " too superstitious" is an unhappy one, for it makes the apostle open his address

---

[1] "Ἄνδρες Ἀθηναῖοι.   [2] δεισιδαιμονεστέρους.

with an assertion which could not but offend his hearers, and it moreover hides from the reader the fine and delicate tact of the speaker by which he at once parries the charge that had been brought against him of being a setter forth of strange gods, and, in doing so, introduces the great truth which he came to preach. The original word answers pretty nearly to our "God-fearing," and may be used either in a good or a bad sense; either to describe the case of those who fear and worship God aright, and so are religious, or that of those who fear God ignorantly and worship Him with gloomy or unholy emotions, and so are superstitious. Perhaps the apostle was not sorry to use a somewhat ambiguous word here, but certainly he did not mean at the very outset of his discourse to make a charge which his hearers would have felt to be an affront.[1] His object was simply to

---

[1] Alford renders the word "carrying your religious reverence very far," and remarks that "blame is neither expressed nor even implied; but their exceeding veneration for religion laid hold of as a *fact*, on which Paul with

lay hold of a fact which furnished him with a basis on which to erect the appeal he intended to make to them. That fact was one which none of them would call in question, and of which it would please rather than offend them to be reminded. Notoriously they were the most religious of all peoples, according to their own notions of religion. This is amply attested by unimpeachable witnesses. A poet of their own says: "If there be any land which knows how to reverence and honour the gods, this surpasses in that."[1] An impartial historian declares, "This is the chief encomium of the city of the Athenians that, in every affair and at all seasons, they follow the gods, and engage in nothing without resorting to prophecy and oracle."[2] Another says of them that they abounded beyond all others in zeal for

exquisite skill engrafts his proof that he is introducing no new gods, but enlightening them with regard to an object of worship on which they were confessedly in the dark." *Greek Test.*, ii. p. 178.

[1] Soph., *Oed. Col.* 1007.

[2] Dionys. Halicar., *De Thucyd. Hist. Judicium*, Sec. 40.

religious rites.¹ And Josephus, the Jewish historian, calls them, in words that furnish an admirable explanation of those of St. Paul, "the most religious of the Hellenes."² In the position, then, with which he starts, the apostle takes them on their own ground, and thus skilfully prepares the way for showing them how, in that very particular in which they thought themselves above all others, they were weak through ignorance and error.

In support of his assertion St. Paul tells them that, in passing through their city, and examining their objects of religious interest —that is, their temples, altars, statues, and rites (not as in the Authorised Version their "devotions")—he came upon an altar on which was the inscription Ἀγνώστῳ Θεῷ, "To an unknown God." Considerable difficulty has been found by some interpreters in reconciling this statement with the absence of all mention of such an altar in Athens

---

¹ Pausan., i. 24. 3.
² *Cont. Apion.* ii. 11 : εὐσεβεστάτους τῶν Ἑλλήνων.

by any ancient writer. But is not the assertion of St. Paul, in an address to the Athenians themselves, amply sufficient to certify the fact without confirmation from any other source? and would it not be preposterous to set aside or call in question the testimony of such a witness simply because no other witnesses can be called to attest the same? But as it happens other witnesses can be adduced; for though no ancient writer makes specific mention of any one altar with this inscription, more than one attest that there were in Athens "altars" to unknown gods.[1] It is certain, then, that such altars existed in Athens, each of them probably bearing the inscription which Paul quotes, and as he had chanced particularly to notice one of them he is naturally led to confine his reference to it.

What did the Athenians mean by such an altar and such an inscription? To this various answers have been given. Some

[1] Pausan. i. 1-3; Philostrat. *Vit. Appolon.* vi. 3, etc See Wetstein on the passage.

have ascribed their erecting it to a vague superstitious dread, which led them to guard against the possibility of provoking the wrath of some deity, of whom they had not heard, by omitting to assign him a place where he might receive honour and homage. But this seems a most improbable suggestion; for had such an idea presented itself to the minds of the Athenians, it could hardly have failed to be followed by the thought that no deity would acknowledge an altar so inscribed, inasmuch as this would be a virtual admission of inferiority and impotence. More probable is the suggestion of those who would attribute the erection of such altars to the consciousness of want and insufficiency which Polytheism leaves upon its votaries; false and baseless, it cannot satisfy the soul of man, so that after he has fancied to himself "gods many and lords many," till he can fancy no more, he still feels an aching void, and gazes forth into the awful infinite, and cries after the unknown. This is true; but is it all that an altar with such an inscription may have been meant to indicate? May we not suppose that in the bosoms of those who erected it there was a deep consciousness that beyond and above all that eye could see, or reason discover, or fancy imagine, there must be a mighty Power on whose will the whole depends, and by whose influence all is pervaded? and unable to form any conception of such a Being, yet having some vague sense of awe and worship, may they not have intended at once to profess their belief and to confess their ignorance by erecting an altar and inscribing to "an unknown God?" I cannot but think that the apostle himself regarded it in this light, else how shall he account for his admission that the God whom he had to declare to them was the very God whom, without knowing Him, they were worshipping? Was not this a distinct acknowledgment that, dim and feeble as was the light that had reached them, it yet was a true ray from the Father of Lights? And is not the whole discourse which the apostle founds on this an endeavour to conduct to a clear and definite consciousness this which he recognised, though in the form but of a vague longing, as a true feeling after God? It seems to me that only on this supposition could the apostle with full truth attach what he had to announce to this inscription; and only thus that the full force of his following argumentation can be felt.

This God whom, without knowing Him, they were worshipping, Paul offers to "declare" unto them. Observe his words. He does not say that he had come to *describe* God to them, or to give them a *just definition* of God, or to help them to form an *adequate conception* of God. No; all that he offers to do is to declare, announce, proclaim to them the true God. And this is all that any of the sacred writers pretend to do; nay, this is all that can be done. For what more can a creature know of God than simply the proclaimed fact of His being and His perfections? "Canst thou by searching find out God? Canst thou find out the Almighty to perfection?"¹ "Dwelling in light which no man can approach unto, no man hath seen Him at any time, or can see Him."² Of His essence and of what He is in Himself we can know nothing. All our thoughts of Him must be relative and analogical—mere reflections and shadows of his unutterable majesty; and only as He reveals Himself to us can we know even this much. For us, therefore, God must ever remain in a most important sense unknown; and as a great philosopher of our own age and country has said, "The last and highest consecration of all true religion must be an altar Ἀγνώστῳ Θεῷ—

To the unknown and unknowable God."³

Happily He who is thus to sense and reason incognoscible hath "declared" Himself to us in such manner as that we may "acquaint ourselves with Him and be at peace." Not only by the works of His hand, which declare

[1] Job xi. 7.   [2] 1 Tim. vi. 16.
[3] Sir William Hamilton, *Discussions*, p. 15.

His glory and show His handiwork, not only in the written record of His character and will in His Word, but most of all in the Person, Mission, Life, and Work of His Son hath He given us a manifestation of Himself which satisfies our religious capacity and is adequate to all the requirements of our spiritual condition. To those who accept this revelation and submit themselves to the mediation of Jesus Christ, the high privilege is secured of seeing God and knowing Him. By Christ we believe in God: He, the only-begotten of the Father, has revealed Him unto us. Through Him we have access unto God: "He hath suffered, the just for the unjust, that He might bring us unto God." We have thus, through Him and in Him, a distinct and impressive realisation of the Infinite and Eternal, whom no man hath seen at any time. We rise above the mere vague belief in a God to the knowledge of the one living and true God. We cease to offer our homage to a mere Power; our hearts open to the recognition of a Personal Deity; and we

IS THE INFINITE THINKABLE? 55

rejoice in the God and Father of our Lord Jesus Christ as our God and our Father through him.[1] The Infinite we frail and finite can never comprehend; but we can believe that He is, and, coming to Him through His Son, we can rest in the assurance that whatever infinite goodness, wisdom, and power can do for us, will be done for us by Him now and for evermore.[2]

APPENDIX TO LECTURE II.

Professor Max Müller on the Notion of the Infinite.

ON such modes of expression as that employed in the text, this very learned and most able writer has recently made some sharp strictures. "The Infinite," says he, "we have been told over and over again, is a negative idea—it excludes only, it does not include anything; nay, we are assured, in the most dogmatic tone, that a finite mind cannot conceive the Infinite. A step further carries us into the very abyss of metaphysics. There is no Infinite, we are told, for there

---

[1] John xx. 17.
[2] See Appendix at the end of this Lecture.

is a Finite—the Infinite has its limit in the Finite, it cannot be Infinite. Now, all this is mere playing on words without thoughts."—*Lectures on the Science of Language*, sec. ser., p. 576. So far as this concluding remark may be intended to apply to what is contained in the sentence preceding, there are few, in this country at least, who will question its justice; though where, in "the abyss of metaphysics," the professor found this piece of unmeaning jargon may be matter of wonder to many. Certain it is, that the philosophers who have asserted man's incapacity to think the Infinite do not so express themselves. They neither deny the existence of the Infinite, nor do they say that because there is a Finite there is no Infinite. What they say is, that the Finite is an object of human knowledge such as man can comprehend in a definite notion, and that from this, man infers the Infinite, though of this he can form no precise notion, but only a vague impression and belief.

Professor Müller continues thus:—"Why is Infinite a negative idea? Because *infinite* is derived from *finis* by means of the negative particle *in*. But this is a mere accident—it is a fact in the history of language, and no more. The same idea may be expressed by the Perfect, the Eternal, the Self-Existing, which are positive terms, or contain at least no negative element." On this I would remark—1. That I am not aware that it has ever been maintained by any one that Infinite is a negative idea *because* the word infinite is formed from *finis* by means of *in*;

nor can I conceive of any one who understands what he means maintaining anything so absurd. The utmost, I suppose, any one has ever said in this direction is, that infinite being a negative concept, it is properly designated by a word expressing a negation. 2. It cannot be conceded that Perfect, Eternal, Self-Existing, are words of the same import as Infinite. They are appropriate to the same object; but they assuredly do not convey the same thought. So that, even allowing them to be "positive terms," it will not follow that Infinite is also a positive term. 3. The terms Perfect, Eternal, Self-Existing, though in form positive terms, are in meaning really negative. Of this the Professor may convince himself by attempting to form a just explanation of them without resorting to negations. The Perfect is simply that to which *nothing* is lacking; the Eternal is that which is *without* beginning and *without* end; the Self-Existing is that which does *not* derive its being from any external source. We think these, as we think the Infinite, exclusively, to use the terminology of the old theologians, *per viam negationis*. Even the authority whom the Professor commends to his readers, Roger Bacon, in the very passage which the Professor quotes, is obliged to confirm the Infinite as a negative—" dicitum infinitum . . . . *per negationem corruptionis et non esse.*"

But the most extraordinary part of Professor Müller's remarks follows:—" The true idea of the Infinite is neither a negation nor a modification of any other idea. The Finite, on the contrary, is in reality the limitation or modification of the Infinite; nor is it possible, if we reason in good earnest, to conceive of the Finite in any other sense than as the shadow of the Infinite." According to this we have no positive notion of the finite; but, having a positive notion of the infinite, we arrive at the finite as its correlative (which is what is meant, I presume, by its "shadow") by limiting the infinite; in other words, we first realise a clear notion of something which is without limits, and by limiting that notion, we get at the notion of something which has limits. This, we venture to say, is a doctrine which no man's consciousness will confirm. Every man knows that when his senses present to him a bounded and figured object, he perceives at once that it has limits, that it has a *finis;* and that it is from such perceptions that he gathers up the notion of finitude. The child does not first form a notion of the boundless, and then from that arrive at the notion that the objects around him have bounds. The reverse is the process; everyday experience suggests to us the notion of the finite, and it is only as the correlative of that, by a process of negation, that we arrive at such notions as we have of the Infinite. It is in vain to say, "No finger, no razor, has ever touched the end of anything;" every man knows that he can with his finger trace innumerable objects to their limit, and that a blunter instrument than a razor will suffice to enable him to cut most things into as many lengths, *i.e.* finite pieces, as he wills. *Some* things, it is true, may elude his power in this respect; it may be quite true that "no eye has laid hold of the horizon which divides heaven and earth, or of the line which separates green from yellow, or unites yellow with white;" and it may be no less true that "no ear has ever caught the point where one key enters into another;" but what relevancy has this to the point in question? It is surely not necessary that we should be able to determine the limits of everything in order to know what is meant by having limits. If we can find the limits of anything it will suffice for that.

An ancient heathen, with whose writings St. Paul was not unacquainted, as he quotes from him (1 Cor. xv. 33), has uttered a maxim respecting the attempt "by searching to find out God," which it might be well for some of our modern speculatists to ponder:—

> Τίς ἐστιν ὁ Θεὸς οὐ θέλῃς οὐ μανθάνειν
> Ἀσεβεῖς τὸν οὐ θέλοντα μανθάνειν θέλων.
>
> Menander, *ex incert. Comoed.*

"Do not will to learn who God is; thou actest profanely in seeking to learn Him when He wills not," *i.e.*, in so far as He has not been pleased to reveal Himself. Another Greek poet tells us that all searching to find out God is vain, and those who attempt this will only have their labour for their pains:

> Θεὸν νομίζε καὶ σέβου, ζήτει δὲ μὴ
> Πλεῖον γὰρ οὐδὲν ἄλλο ἢ ζητεῖν ἔχεις.
>
> Philemon, *ex incert. Comoed.*

III.

St. Paul's Discourse—God and the Universe.

The apostle, recognising the religious principle which lay at the basis of the Hellenic idolatry, but which Polytheism could not satisfy, commences his discourse on the Areopagus by proposing to make known to the Athenians that God whom, without knowing Him, they were worshipping. He offers no proof of a divine existence, which would have been superfluous in addressing an audience the religiousness of which he has already admitted; nor does he attempt to explain to them the divine nature, so as to make God comprehensible by human reason, which he knew to be impossible; he simply offers to " declare " God to them, so as to give an objective reality to their inner convictions, and to satisfy their longings after God with a just and true presentation of Him, so far as He has made Himself known to us, and so far as it is possible for us to apprehend Him. In doing this Paul shows an intimate acquaintance with the state of the Hellenic mind on such subjects, and goes at once to throw the light of revelation on those points on which Hellenic belief and speculation had most completely erred from the truth, and got bewildered and lost. With his announcements concerning God he also combines some declarations concerning man, calculated at once to correct some of the prevailing notions of the Athenians on this head, and to awaken their consciences to a just consideration of their own relations to God. He thus, taking them on their own ground, seeks to bring them under the power of that message of which he was the herald; and from the platform of Natural Religion, on which alone they and he could find a common footing at the outset, to conduct them to that higher and more special revelation of God which he has given by means of "holy men," who "spake as they were moved by the Holy Ghost."[1]

The apostle begins by asserting the creation of all things by God. God, he says, "hath made the world and all things that are in it." By "the world" here Paul does not intend merely the globe which we inhabit; the word he uses, *Cosmos* (κόσμος), is one which the title of a famous work of science, published within these few years, has made familiar to all as a term for the ordered universe.[2] By the Greeks this term was employed properly to denote the universe as under law, and reduced to steadfastness and regular order, as opposed to a state of chaos; and though the classical writers sometimes use it to denote the heavens, its proper meaning always remained present to the Greek mind. To the Greeks the Cosmos

[1] 2 Peter i. 21.
[2] COSMOS: *Sketch of a Physical Description of the Universe.* By Alexander von Humboldt.

was pre-eminently as Aristotle defines it, "the system of heaven and earth and all natures embraced by these."[1] In the New Testament the word is frequently restricted to that part of the ordered universe which we inhabit; but in other passages, besides that before us, it is employed in its proper sense as denoting that universe as a whole. The application of the word to the earth is the result of a Hebraistic influence; in addressing the Athenians Paul would of course use the word in the sense in which it would be understood by them.

The Greeks speculated much concerning the universe; but the idea of *creation* was one with which they were not familiar. Some of their philosophers believed in the eternity of matter; others dreamt of a fortuitous concourse of atoms, out of which all forms came to be arranged by a sort of happy chance; while others taught that there was a world-soul that dwelt in the heart of the

---

[1] Κόσμος ἐστὶ σύστημα ἐξ οὐρανοῦ καὶ γῆς καὶ τῶν ἐν τούτοις περιεχομένων φύσεων. *De Mundo,* sub. init.

mass, and moved, moulded, and governed it. In the popular mind there was simply a confused sense of a gradation of Being from man up through heroes and demigods, and gods of the lesser rank, and gods of the higher, all beings like man, whose existence had had a beginning, and of whose descent it was possible to write a history—what they called a Theogony. In what this series terminated no man could tell; all that the Theogonists could venture to affirm was that Chaos was first, and from it sprang Erebus and black Night, the parents of Aether and Day.[1] Even the highest gods, those who possessed the "many-valleyed Olympus,"[2] were supposed to have had a beginning. The idea of an Infinite and Eternal Essence, by whom all things were made, seems hardly to have entered the popular mind. Even such a sublime thinker as Plato, though he reached to the conception of an eternally existing

---

[1] Hesiod, *Theogon.*, 116-123.
[2] πολύπτυχος Ολυμπος, Hom., *Il.* viii. 4-11; Hes., *Theog.*, 115, *seq.*

being,[1] and asserted that everything capable of being apprehended by the senses must have come into being and had an author,[2] yet seems to have been unable to rise higher than the conception of a Demiurge, or Supreme Arranger of the primary matter, according to an image or paradigm of an absolutely perfect world; and indeed he confesses "that to discover the Maker and Father of the universe is difficult;" and adds, "that when discovered, it is impossible to speak of Him to all."[3] The clear penetrating mind of Aristotle enabled him to reach the definite conception of a First Cause, a First Mover, who must be intelligent, immutable, and perfectly blessed, whom he represented as pure actuality, the thought of thought, the unity of the knowing and the known; but even he could not preserve himself from perplexity and inconsistency, for he maintains that the Cosmos is also eternal and immutable, and it may be doubted

---

[1] τὸ ὂν ἀεί, γένεσιν δὲ οὐκ ἔχον. *Tim.*, p. 27, D.
[2] Ibid. [3] *Tim.* p. 28, C.

if, in his highest conception of God, he rose above the idea of an immanent world-principle not really distinguishable from the world itself.[1] As respects the philosophers of the Epicurean and Stoic sects, to whom belonged those who at this time surrounded Paul, they were wholly in the dark upon this subject. By the Epicureans it was believed that the universe, being full of disorder and misery, could not be the work of an intelligent cause; that it was the result of a fortuitous aggregation of atoms; and that the idea of its being made by the gods was incompatible with just views of them as beings whose felicity consists in eternal repose, and who, having a changeless existence in the space between the worlds, do nothing, and do not create, either by themselves or through the medium of others. The Stoics, on the other hand, whilst they accused the Epicureans of Atheism, and whilst they held the existence of the Deity, were not much nearer

---

[1] Arist. *Metaphys.* xi. 7, p. 1072 B.; *Polit.* vi. 1, etc. Comp. Meiners, *Historia Doctr. De Vero Deo*, sec. 7.

anything like just views of His relation to the world as its Creator; for they taught that matter was eternal as well as God, and that, as all real existences are corporeal, God also is so, though in the refined form of fire. With them God was a dominant power within the world, not a personal existence outside it and distinct from it, by whom it had been made.[1] When the philosophers were thus in the dark, we need not wonder that from among the mass of the people the idea of a creation of the world by God had utterly disappeared.

To us, accustomed from our infancy to ascribe the existence of the universe to God, it may appear strange that, in the minds of intelligent and inquiring persons, as these Athenians were, even though heathens, so much error, obscurity, and ignorance should have existed on this point. Now, that they were not without blame for this is not to be denied; for, as the apostle teaches elsewhere, there is no man who is left without a reve-

[1] Schwegler, *Geschichte der Philosophie*, sec. 17 and 18.

lation of God, the visible creation being a constant witness for the power and divinity of Him by whom it has been made; so that they who, notwithstanding this showing to them of what is known of God, refuse or neglect to acknowledge Him as the Creator of all things, are without excuse.[1] At the same time, it is not surprising that ignorance or error on this point should exist where men are not favoured with an authoritative message regarding it from God. It is to be remembered that the fact of creation is one which transcends the sphere of our experience; and that, even when the fact is made known to us, we are quite unable to realise it in thought. We can conceive neither a Being who has had no beginning, nor a Being who has absolutely begun to be. We speak of the eternity of God, but, except as a negation of any commencement of being, we attach no definite idea to the words. How can we, who are but of yesterday, rise to the conception of a Being who

[1] Rom. i. 20.

stretches away amid the obscurities of an unrevealed past, and never reaches a limit? "Could we," says Dr. Chalmers, "by any number of successive strides, at length reach the fountain-head of duration, our spirits might be at rest. But to think of duration as having no fountain-head; to think of time with no beginning; to uplift the imagination along the heights of an antiquity which hath positively no summit; to soar these upward steeps till, dizzied by the altitude, we can keep no longer on the wing; for the mind to make these repeated flights from one pinnacle to another, and, instead of scaling the mysterious elevation, to lie baffled at its foot, or lose itself among the far, the long-withdrawing recesses of that primeval distance, which at length merges away into a fathomless unknown: this is an exercise utterly discomfiting to the puny faculties of man. We are called on," he adds, "to stir ourselves up that we may take hold of God; but the 'clouds and darkness which are round about Him' seem to repel the enterprise as hopeless; and man, as if overborne by a sense of littleness, feels as if nothing can be done but to make prostrate obeisance of all his faculties before Him."[1] But to this conclusion man will come only if his heart is right with God and he delights to adore where he cannot comprehend. It will be different, where the fear of God has ceased to predominate in men's minds, and where they "like not to retain the knowledge of Him" in their hearts. With such the impossibility of realising the divine eternity will furnish motive sufficient for relinquishing belief in it altogether; and so men will pass easily to a belief in gods who have begun to be, and will relieve themselves from all perplexing questions by relinquishing the universe to the primal domain of Chaos, Erebus, and black Night.

The mind, unable to think of a Being who has never begun to be, is equally unable to think this Being as beginning to create, or as creating in the proper sense of the term.

[1] *Natural Theology*, ch. i., *Works*, vol. i., p. 18.

How are we to conceive of God, with whom there is no change, as passing out of the solitude of his own eternity to commence filling unpeopled space with existence? Whether we ascribe creation to the action of intelligence or to the promptings of benevolence, it is alike impossible for us to understand how He who inhabiteth eternity should have begun in time, or more properly, as Augustine teaches us, *with* time,[1] to obey these impulses. And what idea have we of creation? Men say it is the bringing of something out of nothing; but these are really words that convey no meaning; for that the sum of being in the universe should be increased out of not-being is a position utterly inconceivable by us. The Bible describes it as "a calling of things which are not so as that they are;"[2] but this very language seems to imply a *previous* existence of the things, for how can that be called which does not exist? A thoughtful writer has

[1] Non est mundus factus *in* tempore sed *cum* tempore.— De Civit. Dei, xi. 6.   [2] Rom. iv. 17.

suggested that the things to which the apostle refers are "the eternal possibilities of the divine will,"[1] and that the apostle represents God as calling these into actual realisation. This comes very near to the doctrine of a late eminent philosopher of our own age and country, who says, in reply to the question, What is our thought of creation? "It is not a thought of the mere springing of nothing into something. On the contrary, creation is conceived and is by us conceivable, only as the evolution of existence from possibility into actuality by the fiat of the Deity;" and in a note he adds, "The Divine fiat was the proximate cause of the creation; and thus Deity, containing the cause, contained potentially the effect."[2] But this, though it is the proper statement of the case, and as such throws light on the apostle's words, leaves the subject itself in as great obscurity as ever. The subject, in fact, is beyond our reach. We must be content to

---

[1] Martensen, *Christliche Dogmatik*, sec. 61.
[2] Sir W. Hamilton, *Discussions*, p. 620.

receive the fact on competent evidence, simply as a fact, without comprehending it; our highest philosophy but proclaims our ignorance, and bids us be humble. But if men will not be humble, if they will speculate within a sphere which is too high for them, what wonder that they should go sadly astray, mistaking the meteor-glimmer of their own imagination for the true light, until they are hopelessly bewildered, if not utterly lost?

But though men, through the influence of ungodliness, are led astray in their conceptions of God and his relation to the universe, they still retain their original capacity for receiving the truth on these subjects, and they still have within them a consciousness of God which impels them to worship and trust. To this it is to be ascribed that when men, through disliking to retain the knowledge of God in their thoughts, turned aside from Him, they swerved into idolatry and not into Atheism. To the ungodly heart the most satisfactory assurance would be that which the latter offers, "that there is no God."[1] But from such an assurance man's nature—his rational as well as his moral and instinctive nature—recoils; and it takes a long process of intellectual hardening and familiarity with sophistry to induce any one to regard it with favour. Idolatry, on the contrary, however irrational in itself, does not so directly shock the religious instincts of man; it rather seems to foster and favour them; and as it at the same time relieves man from such thoughts of God, in his majesty, purity, and power, as he desires not to retain, it has caught in its snare the entire race, with the exception of those to whom a verbal revelation has been sent from God. In recognising the religious nature of man, however, and in providing for it, idolatry preserves the means of its own overthrow; for it leaves open the way of access to man's soul for the message of truth when God is pleased to send it, and lays a platform on which those who have to declare to men the

[1] Psalm xiv. 1.

true God can at once take their stand. Of this St. Paul availed himself in his address to the Athenians. When he proclaimed to them that "God made the world and all things that are therein," and that "He is Lord of heaven and earth," he felt assured that the mere announcement of the truth would flash conviction on the minds of his hearers, and would find a response in the indelible feelings of their hearts.

The words in which the apostle's statement here is contained are few, but they have a wide significancy as relating to the religious beliefs and usages of those to whom they were addressed. Not only did they throw a luminous ray across the darkness and confusion which characterised their notions of the universe, but in them he proclaimed the Unity of the Godhead, and the sole lordship of the one God over the universe He had framed. "God that made the world and all things therein :" Here is an emphatic denial of all polytheistic and dualistic notions as to the origin and government of the world—there is but one God, and by Him alone have all things been made that are within the compass of the ordered universe. "God *made* the world:" Here is an emphatic assertion that God is distinct from Nature; that neither is the universe in its totality God, nor is it an emanation from Him, nor is it the mere outward investiture of Him who, as its Mind or Soul, informs and moves it; it is a *product* of His plastic hand, a thing which He has made distinct from Himself, even as an artificer might make something for use or for ornament by his fellowmen. God "is *Lord* of heaven and earth:" Here is an assertion of the sole supremacy of God over the universe He has framed; that which His hand has made His hand alone possesses and upholds; so that "the lords many," amongst whom the Greeks believed that the presidency and control of the universe are distributed, were but the idle creations of fancy, or a vain attempt to relieve man of the vast idea of a superintending Providence, by representing the government of Heaven as analogous to that of an earthly monarch who, unable to survey his large domain, or to conduct its affairs himself, allots it to deputies and satraps, by whom its affairs are administered. By these few words, which first fell from his lips on this occasion, the apostle boldly pushed aside a whole host of errors to which the Athenians had given place in their minds, and by which they had been bewildered and injured. With a vigorous hand he, as it were, swept from the firmament of their religious consciousness the clouds that had been hanging dark and saddening over it, and let the pure bright light of truth, which had been all the while shining behind the veil, flash upon their minds. For a fantastic, though poetical mythology, he gave them a true revelation of God; for an idle and frivolous Theogony, on which some even of their own philosophers had cried shame,[1] he gave them a true and strong Theology, from which the most enlightened philosophers may learn lessons,

[1] Plato, *De Republica*, p. 377, ff.

and of which the highest philosophy may be proud to be the minister.

The apostle leaves these inferences to be drawn from his position by his hearers for themselves; there are two others, of a more practical kind, which he formally announces and presses on their attention. Of these the former is, that God is not to be worshipped through the medium of what is merely outward; the other is, that God is supremely independent of man's worship, and needs no service at his hand. On both these points the Athenians were under the influence of deep and blinding error.

When they erected a temple to any of their gods, they spent on it all the skill and treasure they could command, not with a view of rendering it more commodious for the worshippers, or more adapted to the ends of worship, or more productive of a good religious result by heightening the devotional feeling of the people by whom it was frequented; but because they thought in this way to gratify the god and render him propitious to them. With the same view they called in the aid of sculpture to make beautiful representations of the gods—imagining that they thereby paid a compliment to the deity, and would induce him to be present in his representative when they came to pray to him. We need not suppose that they seriously thought that the deity inhabited the temple as a man might a house, or that the statue of marble or bronze or wood before which they bent was the god; but they did think that it was only through such means that he could be worshipped, and that by the providing of such means their interest with him could be advanced. Closely connected with this is the other error on which the apostle here animadverts: that, namely, of supposing that a man could be "profitable to God" by giving to Him something that He needed. Not only were these splendid temples and beautiful statues intended as gifts to propitiate towards the donor the favour of the deity; still grosser notions had hold of the minds of the people: they thought that the gods had wants which man was capable of supplying, and that by costly offerings and rich sacrifices they not only expressed their homage, but actually effected a claim upon the deity by the benefits conferred on him by their gifts.[1] Religion was thus made wholly an outward thing—a matter of rites and ceremonies—a transaction of barter and exchange between the worshipper and the deity. The idea of a communion between the soul and God, expressing itself in humble contrition for sin and loving trustfulness for grace and blessing on the part of man, and of compassionate tenderness, gracious condescension, and rich unmerited beneficence on the part of God, had almost entirely vanished from their minds. Here and there one more enlightened than the rest might be heard reclaiming against the gross notions by which the multitude were ensnared, and proclaiming that God needed not human ministrations, and that whosoever

[1] See Hom. *Il.*, i. 39-42.

did homage to God as needing anything, forgot that, by so doing, he virtually pronounced himself better than God;[1] but on the mass of the people these voices fell without effect; for them the temple was still the cherished, the necessary dwelling-place of the deity, and the costly offering the proper and indispensable means of procuring his favour. How could it be otherwise so long as the primary falsehood remained which denied the unity, the sole supremacy, and the spirituality of God? If men are taught to believe in "gods many and lords many," if they are taught to regard the universe as not God's creature, and to view it as not under his sole control, but as under the management of a hierarchy of collateral or dependent powers, it is vain to declaim against the grossness of idolatry or the vanity of outward and mercenary worship.

[1] Ipsa [Divûm natura] suis pollens opibus, nihil indiga nostri. Lucret. I. 57. ὅστις τιμᾷ τὸν θεὸν ὡς προσδεόμενον, οὗτος λέληθεν οἰόμενος ἑαυτὸν τοῦ θεοῦ εἶναι κρείττονα. Hierocles *in Carm. Aur. Pythagor.* p. 25.

However obvious this may appear to reason, the mind, obscured and perplexed by fundamental error as to the being and perfections of God, is not in a fit state to feel the force of the appeal.

Clearly perceiving this, the apostle proclaimed to these idolatrous Athenians first of all that One God who made the world and is Lord of heaven and earth; and then he pressed upon them the inference that to think of such a Being as one who could seek for accommodation in an earthly temple, or stand in need of help from human hands, is simply absurd. The apostle enters into no lengthened argument against idolatry, nor does he indulge in any scornful or bitter ridicule of idolatry, as he might legitimately have done, after the example of the ancient prophets,[1] and as several of the Christian Fathers of a later age have done;[2] he con-

---

[1] Comp. Is. xliv. 9-20; Jer. x. 3-5; Hab. ii. 18, 19.
[2] See Tertullian, *Apol.* c. 10-16; Cyprian, *De Vanitate Idolorum*; Arnobius, *Contr. Gentes;* Augustine, *De Civitate Dei.*

tents himself with a calm appeal to the reason of his hearers, after he has set before them the true perfections of God in relation to the universe. Was not such an appeal enough? Having cleared away the error that was the parent of all their other errors in religion, what more was required for his purpose than an appeal to the common sense of the intelligent audience he had before him?

The inference which St. Paul drew as to the absurdity of supposing that a Being such as he declared God to be could be worshipped by men's hands, as if He needed anything, is made by him the point of transition to another part of his declaration—that in which he sets forth the relation of God to man as a Father. To the consideration of this branch of the apostle's discourse we shall proceed in next Lecture.

The truths concerning God, which the apostle brings into prominence in that part of his discourse which we have been studying, are His Unity and His Spirituality.

The Divine Unity is a doctrine with

which all the phenomena of the natural world, rightly interpreted, fall in, but which is certified to us by the written revelation alone. Apart from this, there is so much to be said on both sides by the theology of nature, that a solid and settled belief in the divine unity seems unattainable by those who have no other guide but that, and in point of fact never has been possessed by such. Where men have been able to rise to the conception of God as the Absolute and Infinite, they have of necessity been constrained to think of Him as a monadic essence; for there cannot be two Absolutes or Infinites. But to such conceptions of God only a very few of the higher spirits among the heathen have ever approached. It is the Bible alone that proclaims to us, in a way to reach the convictions of mankind, the great truth that there is but one God. This it does repeatedly and emphatically and in various forms,[1] thereby

---

[1] See Deut. iv. 35, 39; vi. 4; Is. xiv. 5, 6, 18; xliv. 8; John xvii. 3; 1 Cor. viii. 4, etc.

supplementing the conclusions of natural reason, and giving form and substance to those indications which nature supplies of this great truth, but which, without such dogmatical teaching as the Bible furnishes, must ever remain uncertain and unimpressive.

The same may be said of the doctrine of the Divine Spirituality. To this doctrine, when dogmatically enunciated, reason at once responds; for it is impossible to recognise a Being as Independent, Infinite, Eternal, and Omnipotent, otherwise than under the supposition of His being pure Spirit. But experience amply shows that man, left to himself, cannot so think of God. Himself surrounded by materialism and limited, he cannot raise his mind to the conception of an immaterial Being—a Being without parts, without limits, without form, without appreciable relations to space; and hence he invariably attributes to his deity a bodily shape, and sinks gradually into idolatry. It is the firm, emphatic, abiding enunciation of the Divine Spirituality in the written Word which alone preserves the belief of this in the minds of men—one beneficial result among many, of our possessing what some have contemptuously depreciated as a " Book-Revelation."

IV.

St. Paul's Discourse—The Fatherhood of God.

As the apostle surveyed the buildings of Athens, whether during his walks through the city, or as he beheld it stretched out before him from the summit of the Areopagus, he might probably be struck with the contrast which the provision for the public and the religious life of the citizens presented to that which existed for their domestic life or individual well-being. On every side he might behold what was intended to exalt the gods and glorify the people; but for man, as man, little would seem to be cared, and but little done for his comfort. Amidst all the costly and splendid edifices which rose before his view, he would discover none that were devoted to the cause of humanity—no hospitals for the sick, no refuge for the destitute, no asylum for the insane, no home for the orphan.[1] Even the dwellings of the inhabitants presented an aspect of meanness and discomfort which, in a people so skilled in architecture, bespoke an utter disregard of the ordinary comforts of civilised life. The streets in which the people dwelt were narrow, irregular, and ill-paved; their shops were mere open, unglazed booths; and even the abodes of the most wealthy and most noble were immensely inferior to those with which the apostle, coming from Palestine and Asia Minor, would be familiar as occupied by persons of much inferior rank.[2] May we not say that,

[1] An exception must be made to this general statement in respect of the provision made by the Athenians for the education of orphans whose fathers had fallen in war (Plato, *Menexen.* p. 248 D.; Diog. Laert. I. 55; Thucyd. Bk. II. chap. 35, 43, 46). These were brought up at the public expense till they were twenty years of age, after which they received military appointments. If, however, we may believe Aristophanes, this was not always very faithfully done; Cf. *Thesmoph.* 449, *seq.*

[2] Wordsworth, *Athens and Attica*, p. 57.

in the contrast thus glaringly exhibited, there was a sort of typical representation of the tendency and operation of idolatry, which, whilst it lowers the divine by representing it as a mere idealised humanity, utterly overrides the human, and defrauds man of his best rights, his truest dignity, and his purest enjoyments?

Whether the apostle noticed this anomaly or not, his discourse shows that he recognised in the idolatry of the Athenians false and misleading conceptions of men, as well as ignorant and dishonouring conceptions of God. In proclaiming to them, then, the truth, he had to correct the one set of errors as well as the other; and as the two were offshoots of the same stock, and were closely intertwined with each other, his discourse touches sometimes on the one and sometimes on the other. His doctrine concerning man is presented to us as involved in just views of God's relation to man as a Father, as a Governor, and as a Judge.

The conception of God as a FATHER

was not altogether strange to the ancient heathens. The apostle in this discourse cites witnesses from amongst themselves to the fact of the divine paternity :—" As certain of your own poets have said, For we are his offspring." The words quoted by the apostle are to be found in two ancient poems still extant, the Phænomena of Aratus, who was a native of Paul's own province of Cilicia; and the Hymn to Jove, of Cleanthes, who was a native of Assos, in Mysia.[1] With both of their writings the apostle was probably familiar—it may be, more so than many of those who then surrounded him; and this may be the reason why he took a citation from them, when there were so many of the poets whom the Athenians would more heartily have acknowledged as their "own," by whom the same sentiment had been uttered.[2] In any case, the

[1] The words of Aratus are exactly those cited by the apostle—τοῦ γὰρ καὶ γένος ἐσμέν, *Phænom.* 5. Those of Cleanthes are—ἐκ σοῦ γὰρ γένος ἐσμέν, *Hymn. ad Jov.* 5.

[2] See Wetstein on the passage, and Professor Max

apostle's quotation must be regarded in the light of an accommodation; for by none of the Greek poets was the sentiment uttered in the same sense as that in which he applies it here. With them it was used of their fabled deity Zeus or Jupiter, or vaguely of the gods in general; nor did they attach to it any very definite idea of the actual relation in which man thus stood to the higher existences. In the utterance, however, of such a sentiment, the apostle saw the concession, in words at least, of the truth he wished to enforce, and he skilfully lays hold of this to conduct his hearers to the full and intelligent apprehension of it.

The apostle illustrates the Fatherhood of God as manifested in the creation and sustenance of mankind. "He giveth to all," he says, "life, and breath, and all things;" and this more general statement he reiterates more particularly when he asserts that "God made of one blood all nations of men for

* Müller, *Lectures on the Science of Language*, Sec. Ser., p. 459, Cf.

to dwell on all the face of the earth," and that "in Him we live and move and have our being." In these assertions the apostle not only struck at the pride and error of the Athenians, who boasted of themselves that they were Autochthones, sprung from the soil on which they dwelt; but he also denounced the notion, then common among all nations, that each people had a peculiar and independent origin, and so that there was no common bond of humanity uniting the race. He set himself also directly against the opinion so agreeable apparently to the natural mind, that man is sufficient for himself, or, if he depends upon a higher power, it is only as one man may depend on another, whose offices he may secure by some reciprocal service or compensatory gift. Leaving the subject of the unity of the human race for separate investigation, let us at present dwell for a little on the general truth brought before us by the apostle, that God is the Father of all, as the Creator and Preserver of all.

God can be represented to our minds only by similitudes and analogies; and these can never express what He is in Himself, but only what He is in relation to His creatures. Now, in relation to His intelligent creatures, no similitudes can more vividly represent God to us than such as are drawn from the various relations of dependence which men sustain to each other. Accordingly, it is of these the sacred writers and teachers chiefly make use in seeking to convey just views of Him whom they were commissioned and aided by Himself to make known to men—speaking of Him to us as a King, as a Guide, as a Leader, as a Provider, but most of all as a Father.

It is easy to discover on what analogies this representation of God is founded. As an earthly father is the instrumental source of his child's existence, and as it is one of the first duties of a parent to provide for the sustenance, protection, and well-being of his children, so He, who is the real author of our being, and from whose exhaustless bounty all our supplies are drawn, expresses the relation in which we thus stand to Him by calling Himself our Father. The term, consequently, as thus used, is a figurative one. The figure employed, however, not only expresses a *reality*, but of this it is so just and close an expression, that it almost ceases to be a figure, and becomes a direct enunciation of an actual fact.

God is the Father of mankind as the Creator of man. "Have we not all one Father?" asks the Prophet Malachi; "hath not one God created us?"[1] where the paternal character of God is placed in parallel with His relation to us as our Creator. To the same effect is the representation of the apostle here in his address to the Athenians; he derives the relation in which man stands to God as his Father from the fact that God made all men, and that in Him all men live, and move, and have their being. It is not, however, the mere fact of creation that lies at the basis of this relation. If this were all,

[1] Mal. ii. 10.

God might be called the Father of all inanimate as well as animated beings, whereas the term is applied to Him only in his relation to intelligent creatures. In Scripture only angels and men are called sons of God; and I do not know that even among the heathen the fatherhood of their supreme god was conceived of as extending beyond inferior gods and men, save as it was involved in vague pantheistic notions of an all-pervading influence, the source of universal life in nature. Certainly it was in his relation to intelligent beings alone that the highest artistic embodiment of the Greek conception of their supreme god was produced, in the famous statue of Phidias, on which the Athenians gazed with unceasing reverence, and not to have seen which was held to be one of the greatest of calamities.[1] All this points to a consciousness on the part of man of a relation to God higher than that of mere creation—a relation which has to do with man as possessed of reason and a moral sense. Man

[1] Müller, *Ancient Art*, pp. 75, 362, Leitch's Translation.

feels that, thus endowed, he is not only raised infinitely above the brutes that perish, but that there is in some sense an affinity thereby established between him and the Being of beings whom he worships. The truth of this the Bible fully recognises, and in the Bible alone do we find its real basis and true expression. God is our Father, not only as the former of our bodies, but especially and supremely as the Author to us of intelligence and moral discrimination. He is emphatically "the Father of Spirits," by subjection to whom we live—"the God of the spirits of all flesh,"[1] in whose hand all beings are. And all this falls back on the original account of man's creation, where we are told not only that after God had fashioned man of the dust of the earth, He "breathed into him the breath of life and man became a living soul," but also that, thus brought into existence, man was made in the image and likeness of God.[2] It is on this ground that Adam is emphatically

---

[1] Heb. xii. 9 ; Num. xvi. 22.   [2] Gen. ii. 7 ; i. 27.

called in Scripture "the son of God,[1] as the first on whom was bestowed this sublime gift of standing forth the spiritual representative, image, and analogue of God; and though sin has sadly marred this once fair image, and has robbed it of some of its choicest lines, enough yet remains to raise man above all God's creatures here, and give to his relation to God as his Father a worth and a dignity which mere creation could not confer.

And as God has made us, so it is He who sustains and preserves us from day to day. "He," says the apostle, "giveth us life, and breath, and all things. In Him we live and move, and have our being." All the faculties of life, the power to exercise these faculties, and the favourable circumstances by which the exercise of them is rendered easy and pleasant to us, come to us as the gift of God. He has established all those fine adaptations between us and the outer world by means of which our life is sustained

[1] Luke iii. 38.

and innumerable sources of enjoyment are opened to us; and it is His constant care which preserves these adaptations, and maintains the conditions on which our receiving the advantages of them depends. All things, by the uses of which our life is continued and made prosperous, are kept in being and order and utility by Him. He preserveth all things by the word of His power; in His hand is the soul of every living thing, and the breath of all mankind. In Him we *live;* apart from Him our life would decay, and be extinguished as a flame which had been suddenly deprived of its sustaining element. In Him we *move;* apart from Him we are not only inert and helpless, but not even such movement as sustains the life of plants would be possible for us. " In Him we *have our being;*" in Him we are; apart from Him we should not only cease to be what we are, but we should cease to be at all; it is only the hand of God that interposes between us and annihilation. He is thus to us an ever gracious and bountiful Father, watching over us with a ceaseless care and unwearied tenderness; causing His sun to rise upon the evil as well as the good; ever testifying Himself to men, "in that He doeth good and giveth us rain from heaven, and fruitful seasons, filling our hearts with food and gladness."[1]

There is a peculiarity in the language of the apostle in the statement we have been last considering, which must not be slightly passed over. He does not, it will be observed, say, "*by* Him" or "*through* Him," but "*in* Him we live and move and have our being." Now this phraseology must neither be explained away, on the one hand, as if it meant nothing more than that God is to us the author, somehow, of life, and motion, and existence; nor, on the other hand, must we allow ourselves to be persuaded that the apostle's words contain any sanction of that view of God which confounds Him with the creation, or the creation with Him. We are bound to believe that in

[1] Acts xiv. 17.

some sense we have our being *in* God, and not merely *from* Him and *through* Him; and yet we must beware of any view which would lead us to deny or overlook the distinction which personally discriminates us from God. The apostle, we may be sure, would be especially on his guard on this occasion against uttering anything that would seem to give the remotest countenance to such a view; for this was one of the great errors of the Stoics, by some of whom he was at that moment surrounded. What was the apostle's meaning here we may gather from the connection with this of his immediately preceding statement, that God is not far from any one of us. This implies at once proximity and distinction, intimacy of relation, and yet difference of personality; and, in connection with this, we may infer, that the immanence of man's life in God, of which the apostle here speaks, is an immanence, not of nature or essence, but only of relation and effect; that man lives in God, not as if he were one with God, but in the sense that he is so encompassed with the divine influence that he cannot pass beyond it, and so dependent on the divine hand that he cannot exist away from it. " I doubt not," says Calvin, " that Paul means that we are in a sense contained in God, inasmuch as He dwells in us by His virtue. And though God separates himself from all His creatures by the name of Jehovah, that we may know that, properly speaking, He alone is; yet we subsist in Him, inasmuch as He quickens and sustains us by His Spirit. For through all parts of the world is the power of the Spirit diffused, preserving them in their condition, and supplying to heaven and earth the vigour which we see, and to animate beings also motion; not as frenzied men foolishly talk, that all things are full of the gods, nay, that the very stones are gods, but because God, by the marvellous vigour and instinct of His Spirit, preserves whatever He has created."[1] We are thus taught to realise God's preservation of us, not as a result merely of certain

[1] Comment. on this place.

laws and arrangements which He has instituted, and continues in operation for our benefit, but as the consequence of God's constant presence with us, care of us, thought concerning us, and acting for us. It is a favourite notion with many that God governs the world only by general laws; that having organised this universal system, and fitly adjusted all its parts to each other, He has retired from the active control of it, and left it to work on of itself; so that the universe is like a vast machine which has been set a-going, and will continue to go on without intermission by its own inherent forces for ever. But it is not so that either the Bible or a sound philosophy teaches us to view the matter. Whilst it is undoubtedly true, that the universe is under the guidance of great general laws, it is no less true that God has the whole under his immediate control, and regulates the whole according to His own will and plan. The course of nature is uniform; the laws of nature are constant and regular; but this course is elastic, and these laws leave room for the introduction of free and rational agents. Experience teaches us that even we can interpose amid the operation of natural laws, so as to secure results which we desire; how much more, then, may not God so interpose when He sees meet? If man may come in among nature's laws, and without interrupting their action, find scope for affecting his own purposes and carrying out his own thoughts, how much more is this possible for Him, by whom all these laws have been instituted, and who holds the entire universe in His hand? Here, then, is the point at which Faith comes in with her lesson, to supplement those of science and observation. Whilst she recognises the world as a grand machine, she forbids us to believe that all events are brought about by the mere action of natural laws. She reminds us that the world is not left to itself; but that over its material organisation and natural order there presides an infinite and all-potent Mind, for carrying out the purposes and thoughts of which the elasticity of nature affords continual facility. We can thus go forth along our path in the assurance that it is not a blind fate, not an insensate mechanism, not a dead law that determines our affairs; but that God's hand is around us, and God's eye is upon us, and God's counsel is guiding us; that His "thoughts are towards us;" that His mighty Spirit breathes and energises on every side of us; and that thus encompassed by God it is grandly true that "IN HIM we live, and move, and have our being."

As our creator, then, and preserver, God stands to us in the relation of a father. To Him, in this capacity, may we all approach; and to Him, as thus related to us, it behoves us to render reverence and worship. From Him all receive their being, and in Him all continue to exist. His hands have made and fashioned our bodies: it is He who hath formed the spirit within us; and it is by His inspiration that we have understanding.[1] Our position in life, the circumstances of our

[1] Job xxxii. 8.

birth, the growth and training of our inner nature, the events of our entire history, and the varied influences that have moulded and modified our characters, have all been under His control, and have come into operation as He saw meet. It is He who has kept us from the first until now; holding us in the hollow of His hand, and never for one instant, by day or by night, withdrawing from us His watchful eye. The bounty that has supplied all our wants is His. The Providence that has guarded us on many a perilous path, and warded off from us many a destructive blow, and brought smiling to us many a kindly influence, is His. And His is the wisdom-guided finger that has been regulating that vast though unseen working of education and discipline, under whose constant and plastic influence we have been brought, and to which it is mainly owing that we are what we are. To Him, then, it behoves all men to come as to a Father; at His footstool it becomes them to bend as grateful, reverent, and obedient children; to Him ought the sacrifice of thanksgiving and of praise to be offered by all continually; and to His fatherly wisdom, tenderness, and love, ought all to commit their way for what lies before them of the journey of life, assured that if they acknowledge Him in all their ways, He will direct their paths.[1]

In asserting God's fatherhood as the creator and preserver of all men, the apostle had in view, not only the recalling of these Athenians to just thoughts of God, and of their own true worth in relation to Him, but the arousing of their consciences to a sense of sin, in that, being God's offspring, they had "not honoured him as God, neither been thankful."[2] For such neglect of Him and His claims God will not hold men guiltless. "If," said He to the Jews by the prophet, "If I be a father, where is mine honour."[3] This challenge proceeds on the assumption that it is the duty and the natural impulse of a son to honour his father; and God represents Himself as defrauded of that which

[1] Prov. iii. 6.   [2] Rom. i. 21.   [3] Mal. i. 6.

is His due, and his people as following a wicked and unnatural course when they withhold from Him that honour which, as a father, He claims. What He thus said to the Jews by the prophet, He is virtually saying to all men. From all He claims the honour due from a child to a parent, and especially due from man to one so compassionate, bountiful, long-suffering, and gracious as is "our Father who is in heaven;" and when this honour is withheld, be assured that he who is a jealous God, and will not suffer his glory to be given to another, will make inquisition for it, and will ask of each man who hath withheld it, "*Where* is My honour?"

These Athenians had, in their error and ignorance, been giving to graven images that honour and praise which belong only to God. How the apostle convicts them of sin and folly for this we shall afterwards see; in the meanwhile let us look to ourselves, and see whether we are clear of blame in this respect. A man needs not to bow down to stocks and stones, or to offer worship to the work of his own hands, to be an idolator. Whenever the heart is set upon any object with that affection which is due only to God —whenever any pursuit or end engrosses the supreme interest and occupies supremely the active powers of the man so that God is either entirely forgotten, or allowed only a subordinate place in the soul and life— whenever any creature is made an object of trust and confidence, to the exclusion of God, or happiness is sought away from Him, and in disregard of Him—whenever, in short, men put in the place of God that which is not God, there is idolatry; and there is the honour which God claims as a father, wantonly and wickedly withheld. Alas! who of us can pretend to be free from the charge of thus dishonouring our Father? And whilst the consciousness of this should fill us with humiliation and contrition, should not the knowledge that notwithstanding all our rebellion, ingratitude, and impiety, God has still been exercising towards us the offices of a gracious and compassionate Father, carry home to our hearts, with melting power, the conviction of that relation in which He stands to us, and stir up within us the deepest emotions of filial desire and tenderness? Should not the goodness of God, thus manifested to us, be constantly leading us to repentance? Should it not make us long to return to His presence, and yield ourselves to His love? And when, in addition to this, we are assured that He has, at an immeasurable cost—even by the giving up for us of His own Son to die for us—opened a pathway by which we may return to Him, and enter into relations of amity and peace with Him—does not every consideration of duty—does not every emotion of gratitude urge us to hasten to His footstool and embrace His offered mercy?

What impiety can go beyond that of the man who shall harden his heart against such fatherly grace as this? What infatuation can surpass that of the man who, for some carnal enjoyment or some worldly possession, shall despise or neglect the riches of a beneficence so truly divine as this?

Ah then, my hungry soul! which long hast fed
On idle fancies of thy foolish thought;
And, with false beauty's flattering bait misled,
Hast after vain deceitful shadows sought,
Which all are flesh, and now have left thee nought:—
Look up at last unto that Sovereign Light,
From whose pure beams all perfect beauty springs,
That kindleth love in every godly sprite,
Even the love of God; which loathing brings
Of this wide world and those gay-seeming things;
With whose sweet pleasures being so possest,
Thy straying thoughts henceforth for ever rest.
SPENSER.

V.

St. Paul's Discourse—Unity of the Human Race.

THE idea of a universal religion presupposes the unity of the human race, as well as the unity of God. Where polytheistic beliefs prevail, there will naturally prevail along with them the conception of different religious principles, different modes of worship, and different forms of service, as appropriate to different deities, and to the different kinds of relation between the worshipper and his God, arising out of the peculiar character of each deity, or the historical circumstances which are believed to stand connected with his apotheosis. And on the other hand, when men believe that each nation or people has had a separate origin, and that consequently no common tie binds the members of the race generally to each other and to one common father, there will be neither ground nor inclination for such a community of faith and worship as the idea of a universal religion would imply. Hence we find that fellowship in religious acts, and a unity of religion for the race, are purely biblical conceptions of which no trace is to be found either in the traditions or in the usages of polytheistic nations.

It may be further observed that polytheism and a denial of the unity of the human race generally go together. Nor is this to be wondered at; for when men believe in many gods, each nation comes naturally to have its own gods; and where each nation has its own gods, it cannot fail to follow that each nation will trace its origin to the deities it alone believes in and worships. In the minds of the Athenians whom Paul addressed on Mars' hill these erroneous notions were deeply imbedded. Filled with polytheistic beliefs, they regarded each separate people as having sprung from a different source. They knew of no common centre from which all the varieties of men had radiated. They had utterly lost the knowledge of God as the creator and father of the race, and with that all knowledge of the race as one family, the creatures and children of the one God and Father of all. It was needful, therefore, for the apostle, whose purpose it was to lead them to the point where he could, with effect, announce to them the doctrines and claims of Christianity as the one religion for all men, to endeavour to disabuse their minds of the error under which they laboured, regarding the relation of mankind to each other; and, while he proclaimed to them the one God, Lord of heaven and earth, and Father of all mankind, to tell them also that God had "made of one blood all nations of men for to dwell on all the face of the earth."

That the notion of distinct sources for the different nations of the world should rise in men's minds is not surprising; and that it should have universally prevailed in ancient times, when nations had comparatively but little intercourse with each other, and were exposed to all the narrowing and hostile prejudices which this fostered, will appear the less strange when we advert to the fact that in our own day such opinions have not only been promulgated but have found advocates amongst men of science. It must be admitted also, that at first sight the phenomena of the case would almost seem to authorise some such conclusion. Whilst we see man spread over the whole habitable globe, accommodating himself to every climate and thriving on the produce of every zone, we cannot but mark the glaring differences which subsist between the natives of different regions of the globe. If we take the high-bred inhabitant of a European city, and place by his side a Mongolian from Siberia, or a Hottentot from South Africa, the difference between them will be so marked as not to escape the most cursory observer; and if we take these as typical instances we shall find, as we survey the race, a vast variety of intermediate peculiarities which may be ranked under these, but which, viewed by themselves, divide men into classes more or less distinctively marked off from each other. In the presence of such facts, it is hardly possible to resist the inquiry: Are these, which differ so much from each other, beings of the same species? Is the flat-faced tawny Mongolian, with his oblique eyes, prominent cheekbones, retreating forehead, and projecting jaws; or the jet-black negro, with his woolly hair, and the lower part of his face so projecting as to give the head the appearance of being placed "*behind* the face rather than *above* it,"[1]—a being of the same species with the fair-skinned European, with his vertical profile, prominent features, oval countenance and silken hair? Can the rude savage, whose habits are little better than those of the brute, who roams the forest or the desert in a state of nudity, who snatches a precarious meal from the chances of the chase

[1] Latham.

or ekes it out by devouring insects and reptiles, or, it may be, luxuriates in devouring the dead body of his enemy, be pronounced a being of the same nature and kind as the refined well-dressed European, whose food is selected with the most scrupulous nicety, and prepared with scientific dexterity, who seeks a settled abode where he surrounds himself with provident safeguards against the contingencies of the future, whose tastes seek gratifications far beyond those of sense and passion, and who is ever pressing forward in the career of intellectual and physical improvement? Are the differences, so obvious between these, attributable wholly to variety of culture, circumstance, and history; or do they point to some deeper, some constitutional, some ineradicable variety which forbids us to regard the two as beings of the same kind? Have we, in short, in the human animal, one race with varieties of an accidental and superficial kind, or a number of distinct races, each of which has had a separate and peculiar source?

This is a question which has long, and especially of late years, engaged the attention of scientific men. For the student of scripture it has no especial interest, except as he may wish to see harmony preserved between the statements of the Bible and the conclusions of science, and to derive the satisfaction which always accrues from finding that the deliverances of the inspired word are confirmed by the facts which scientific observation collects, and the inferences to which scientific inquirers are led from these. So far as the testimony of scripture goes, there is no scope for diversity of opinion on this question. From beginning to end it never recognises even the possibility of doubt as to the homogeneity of the whole race of man, and the descent of all its members from one pair. Not only have we such express statements as that in Gen. iii. 20, where Adam, doomed to mortality because of sin, yet recognising, through the gospel which had been proclaimed to him, the perpetuity and final triumph of his race, gives utterance to his faith and hope by calling his wife Eve (Hhavvah or Life,[1] *i.e.*, the Vivifier), a name appropriate to her, because she is "the mother of all living," the progenitress of the whole human race; not only have we the apostle, in this discourse, stating expressly to the Athenians "that God hath made of one blood all nations of men to dwell on all the face of the earth;" but the entire history which the Bible gives, and the whole scheme of religious truth which it teaches, proceed on this and no other assumption. No one can read the earlier chapters of Genesis without seeing that they are *meant* by the writer to unfold to us the origin of the human race in the pair whom God placed in Paradise, to whom He gave the whole earth for a possession, and on whom He pronounced the blessing, "Be fruitful and multiply, and replenish the earth, and subdue

[1] חַוָּה from חָוָה, *to breathe, to live.*

it."[1] It is equally plain that at a subsequent period Moses distinctly represents the whole human race as surviving in Noah and his family, and as finding a second progenitor, so to speak, in him.[2] We find him also, at a still later period, representing the race as not only one physically, but as forming only one society and as using only one language; and he mentions an incident to which he clearly traces all the diversities which have since distinguished the classes or nations into which men have been since divided.[3] We find also that the sacred writers unhesitatingly refer certain moral peculiarities of our race, as well as certain spiritual disabilities under which it is placed, to their connection with the first man; and no one can receive his idea of Christianity from the New Testament, without feeling satisfied that, alike by its divine founder and His apostles, it is offered to mankind as belonging to a race which is essenti-

---

[1] Gen. i. 28.   [2] Gen. ix. 1; x. 32.
[3] Gen. xi. 1–9.

ally one, as all involved in one common doom, endowed with the same capacities of being restored, and alike dependent for recovery on "the common salvation." So far, then, as the Bible is concerned, this must be held as a settled question; neither its express statements, nor its general tenor, nor its peculiar doctrines, admit the hypothesis of an essential and original diversity in the different tribes of man.

The question is, therefore, one purely of scientific interest. But is it one which science is competent to settle? On this point men of the profoundest science are found unhesitatingly pronouncing in the negative; and in this I presume to think they are right. Observation may supply them with certain facts, and these facts may fall in better with one hypothesis than with another; but unless it could be scientifically determined what diversities are and what are not compatible with community of origin, science can make no pretence to determine authoritatively this question. It is competent, however, for science to pronounce on the *probabilities* of the case; that is to say with which hypothesis observed facts chiefly accord; and so far it behoves us to listen to the scientific inquirer, and gratefully to accept such trustworthy aid as he may be able to give us towards arriving at some satisfactory conclusion.

Now, when we turn to the writings of those scientific men who have arrived at a general conclusion on this subject, opposed to that which the Bible authorises, it cannot be said that, in the outset, they command respect by the uniformity or concurrence of their views. Here, as in many other departments of science, one is constantly reminded of the remark of Cicero, that there is no opinion so absurd as not to have been advanced by some philosophers;[1] and when one sees the extreme lengths to which inferences are pushed, and the narrow bases on which prodigious conclusions are built, one is led to suspect that prejudice and pas-

[1] *De Divin.* ii. 58.

sion have often had as much to do with the structure as science, if not more. Thus whilst some, from mere haughtiness of self-esteem, repudiate with disdain all community of nature with the more degraded specimens of humanity, and some are spurred to the same conclusion, that they may find an apology for oppressing their fellowmen, and using them as beasts of burden; others, with a startling comprehensiveness of embrace, not only admit the unity of the whole human family, but impute to man a common origin with some of the brutes—affirming with a learned Scottish judge of the last century, that the " ourang-outangs are proved to be of our species, by marks of humanity which are incontestable;"[1] or, with a more recent writer, that man is but the development of a germ, which, at its successive stages, may be frog, fish, monkey, or man.[2] If, again, we follow

---

[1] Monboddo, *Origin of Language*.

[2] *Vestiges of the Nat. Hist. of Creation*; comp. also Darwin's *Origin of Species*, c. xiv. p. 484, and other places. See Appendix to this Lecture.

those who are of opinion that all men are not the descendants of one pair, we are perplexed by the diversity of opinion in which they involve us, as to the number of centres they find for the human race, and as to the actual mode of its formation; some like the first speculator on the subject, the far-famed Rosicrucian Theophrastus Paracelsus, contenting themselves with two Adams, others contending for five, others for twelve—and all resting upon grounds which would equally well support a demand for scores or hundreds; while a living philosopher has put the crown upon this growing absurdity by declaring that "men must have originated in nations as the bees have originated in swarms."[1] From such diversities and extravagances of opinion, it must be very evident that science has little that is *certain* to teach in opposition to the teaching of the Bible on this subject.

It may be observed also, in the outset, that so far as superior intelligence and at-

[1] Agassiz, as cited by Hamilton, *The Pentateuch, etc.*, p. 287

tainment can give authority to a scientific decision, the preponderance in this respect is immensely in favour of the Bible doctrine of the unity of the human race. With a few exceptions, the writers who have adopted the opposite conclusion are men who have not won for themselves a high place or much fame in any department of science; whilst on the other side stand nearly all the great chiefs of modern scientific research and speculation. It may suffice, on the present occasion, to name such men as Buffon, Linnæus, Soemmering, and Cuvier, in natural history; Blumenbach, Müller, and Wagner, in anatomy; Prichard, Latham, Pickering, among ethnologists; Adelung, W. von Humboldt, and Bunsen, among philologists; and Alexander von Humboldt, at whose feet all science had laid down its treasures. These are the names of men who have investigated this subject purely as a question of science; each is a prince in his own department; and all of them, after the most careful study of the subject, have declared, as the only conclusion to which they could come, that all men are of one race or species, and that the Bible account of their origin is that with which alone science can come into harmony.

It is not to be denied, however, that there are *difficulties* in the way of this conclusion—difficulties arising from the varieties which mark the different families or tribes of men scattered over the surface of the globe. But in regard to these it may be remarked, that though it should be found impossible to account for them, or to show *how* they have arisen in the case of beings descended from one pair, it will not follow from that, that the hypothesis of a common origin of the race is scientifically untenable. It may be that these differences of external appearance, and in some cases of structure, are attributable to purely natural causes which may be indicated; or it may be that when God confounded the language of men at Babel, and produced thereby linguistic varieties, which it has not yet been possible to refer to a common type, He, at the same time, caused varieties of the human species to be produced; but whether such modes of accounting for the varieties be possible and admissible or not, the mere fact of these varieties cannot be held as sufficient to invalidate the hypothesis of a common origin of the race, unless it can be shown that the varieties afford stronger reasons for rejecting that hypothesis than the affinities of the human race afford for adopting it. If it shall be found, on inquiry, that the points of identity are more numerous by far than the points of diversity; and that whilst the latter are superficial, and may possibly be attributable to the influence of outward circumstances, the former are essential, belong to man as man, and never could have been produced by any casual or external influence,—it must be felt by all clear and candid minds that the overwhelming weight of probability is in favour of that hypothesis which accords with the teaching of the Bible on this subject.

Now, that this is really the true state of the case may, I think, be made very evident, even without entering very deeply into inquiries which are not suitable for our present engagement. On questions of an anatomical, physiological, and philological kind, we may content ourselves with allowing our judgment to rest very much on the opinions of men to whom these subjects have been familiar from constant and careful study; whilst there are other departments of knowledge bearing on this question, in which we may be fully competent to judge wholly for ourselves.

When anatomy and physiology are questioned on the subject of the unity of the human race, the answer returned is in substance, that whilst diversities of colour in the skin, diversities in the structure of the skeleton, and diversities in the texture of the capillary integuments more or less important, distinguish the human race into varieties, none of these is such as to amount to an obliteration of the specific and original unity of the race; whereas the points of resemblance are so numerous, and so essential, as to speak loudly in favour of that unity. The greatest difficulty here is furnished by the existence of differences in the bony structure of certain nations as compared with others; but the fact that congenital departures from the prevailing type are known to be propagated through wide-spread families in the midst of the so-called races, goes very far to deprive this peculiarity of any power to impeach the doctrine of the original unity of the race; for the skull of the Mongolian, or the extremities of the negro, *may* have originated in some congenital abnormity, which has descended from generation to generation, and so spread over a whole nation. As for peculiarities of the colour and of the hair, these are subject to too many exceptions in existing tribes, and can be shown to be in so many cases materially affected by climate, and food, and general condition, and have been known in so many instances within historical memory to have arisen where they did not before exist; that no stress whatever can be laid on them as proving an original diversity in the human race. On the other hand, we have in all men the same broad and well-defined peculiarities by which man is discriminated from every other species of animals; the same general structure; the same bodily characteristics; the same physical necessities; the same liabilities to bodily injury from the same causes; the same average duration of life, and the same process of growth, maturity, and decay. In the face of such evidences of unity, a few diversities of colour and of form cannot be allowed to raise in our minds any serious objection to that conclusion.

When, from observing man's bodily structure, we pass to the consideration of his inner being, we find the evidence of the unity of the race still more impressive and cogent. All men have the same general mental constitution; the same number of mental faculties; the same methods and processes of acquiring knowledge; the same susceptibilities, emotions, and passions,—the same in kind, I mean, however different they may be in degree. We find also that all men carry on their mental processes in obedience to exactly the same laws; and that these things, which are common to all men, are peculiar to man alone of all animals. Another peculiarity which he has, and which arises out of his mental constitution, is the faculty of speech. This faculty all men possess; and speech is essentially the same process in all. It is also peculiar to man, who alone has organs fitted for such a process, and alone the capacity to turn these to such a use. So remarkable a peculiarity seems of itself to pronounce decisively in favour of the community of our race. By some the argument from language has been pushed even beyond this. Founding on the remarkable inductions of comparative philology, by which languages, apparently quite distinct from each other, have been found not only to stand in affinity, but to be so closely related as to be sisters of one mother tongue, some inquirers have not hesitated to anticipate the time when all the languages of earth shall be shewn to be fundamentally one, and thus irresistibly demonstrate the deduction of all nations from one common source. What has been already accomplished in this direction is so marvellous, that one would be slow to doubt the possibility of such a result as that indicated; still, as it has not yet been attained, and as it is possible that in their upward generalizations, philologists may find themselves stopped at the Tower of Babel, where the confusion of speech that we are told took place by divine interposition, may have amounted to a miraculous construction of several essentially different languages, and not merely to the introduction of dialectical varieties in the one language, I do not feel myself at liberty to lay much stress on this as a *direct* argument for the primitive unity of the race. Collaterally, however, the results of comparative philology contribute in one important respect to this conclusion; they show that nations, the affinity of whose languages proves that originally they were the same tribe, may in process of time come to be so physically diverse from each other, as to be regarded by those who look only on their physical characteristics as belonging to different races; and thus they demonstrate how little weight can be legitimately attached to these physical diversities as bearing on this question. Who, for instance, looking merely at the outward appearance, would suppose that the Greek, the Roman, the German, the Anglo-Saxon, belonged to the same family as the Brahmin of India? or that the Irish and Scottish Celt is of the same original tribe as the Persian or the Hindoo? And yet the former of these is so certain, that no comparative philologist has the slightest doubt of it; and the latter rests on a basis of evidence which, if not definitively convincing, is such as it would not be easy to overthrow.[1]

Advancing a step farther, we come to

[1] See Prichard's *Eastern Origin of the Celtic Nations*, new edition by Latham; and on the subject generally, Prof. Max Müller's *Lectures on the Science of Language*, 1st and 2d series, and Johnes' *Philological Proofs of the Unity of the Race*, etc.

look at man's *moral* and *religious* nature; and here we find the most striking indications of original and fundamental unity pervading the race. Degraded, benighted, and brutalised as vast masses of mankind are; besotted by ignorance, blinded by superstition, polluted and perverted by crime, as many tribes have been for generations, it needs only that we should look a little below the surface to satisfy ourselves that in them there is essentially the same moral nature as exists and operates in the most refined, virtuous, and religious nations. In all there is a sense of the distinction between right and wrong; in all there is an emotion of approval of what is judged to be right, and of condemnation of what is counted wrong; in all there is a conscience, which is constantly either "accusing or else excusing" its possessor in reference to his deeds; and in all there is a sense of obligation, a feeling of responsibility, a reference to a supreme power from whom that obligation proceeds, and to whom that responsibility is due. The standard by which nations judge of moral relations may be very different, and yet the process of moral judging be essentially the same in all; and so, in point of fact, it is found to be.[1] In like manner, the religious beliefs, usages, and tendencies of nations may differ; and yet religion, so far as its mental character and its place in the moral economy is concerned, be essentially the same in all; and so, in point of fact, we find it to be. But the differences here are due to outward circumstances, to the possession or the want of an objective revelation of moral and spiritual truth, to favourable or unfavourable means of moral culture, to historical events, to local position, and to many causes of a purely outward and casual nature; whereas the points of agreement are found attaching to man's inner nature, and is therefore essentially characteristic of him. Who does not see how forcibly this concludes for the inherent unity of the race? how it is, in fact, an echo coming back from man's own

[1] Art. *Moral Philosophy*, in the *Encycl. Brit.*, vol. xv. p. 541.

bosom to the inspired assertion that God "hath made of one blood all nations of men for to dwell on the face of all the earth."— And here I may notice that the comparison of different religions professed among men has led to much the same result as the comparison of different languages. Affinities between the religious traditions and usages of the most different and apparently unconnected tribes have been shown to exist, pointing to a time when these tribes lived in a common home and professed a common faith; and the hope has been expressed, that further investigation may justify the conclusion that all the heathen mythologies, ancient and modern, are only corruptions, more or less extensive, of that primitive faith which the first man taught to his children, and of which we have the correct tradition and perfected form in the Bible. This inquiry, however, has not yet been prosecuted sufficiently to justify us in taking from it any positions to be used argumentatively in such an investigation as that in which we are engaged. Collaterally, however, it is valid for the same use as that to which we have already applied the facts furnished by comparative philology; and the two together not only go in the same direction, but mutually confirm and supplement each other; so that we may entertain the hope that when both have been more thoroughly explored, the result will be such as to lend fresh evidence and illustration of the truth of what the Bible teaches as to the unity of the human race.

In the meantime, it is satisfactory to know that science has not only nothing to advance distinctly incompatible with this belief, but that its various streams of testimony appear to converge towards the scientific establishment of it. The friends of the Bible need not be greatly moved, therefore, by the new and strange hypotheses which, in our own day, are so freely ventilated, as to the origin of the human race, and which are so utterly irreconcilable with the testimony of Scripture upon the subject. Let us distinguish between what science can *prove*, and what men of science can *ingeniously fancy and adroitly expound;* and, so long as we find that it is only within the sphere of the latter that doctrines adverse to the Bible are advanced, we may remain at ease and await the time when what only fancy has created, true science will indignantly put aside. Remembering that the maxim of the great Newton was, "Hypotheses non fingo"—"I feign not hypotheses;" and being confident that the principle which guided him is still that which guides the great chiefs of science in this country, we may rest assured that its supremacy will be asserted to the discomfiture of that tendency towards mere hypothesis which has of late so much usurped over true scientific inquiry both here and on the continent.

With the assertion of the unity of the human race the apostle completes what he had to teach to these Athenians concerning the general fact of the fatherhood of God over the race. Not only has God made all men, so that they are, in virtue of their being, His sons; but He has made all of one blood,—all partakers of the same nature, and akin to each other as descended from the same source. These two positions, though they are complements of one great whole, are independent of each other. The fact that all men are God's creatures and children, does not necessarily involve the fact that the entire human race is of one blood; for God, had He seen meet, might have formed mankind at different centres, as we find he has formed the lower animals. The unity of the human race, therefore, required to be asserted by the apostle as a distinct and further proposition; and this he does in language which, we may well believe, would startle and astonish those whom he addressed. In this way, however, he laid broad and deep the basis on which he could advance and unfold to them that message of authority and of grace with which he was charged. Only on the ground of a common creation by God, and a community of nature and blood, could he, a Jew, have any title to demand the attention of those Greeks to a message purporting to relate to their religious interests and welfare. If God had not made them, as well as him, what claim had his God on their attention? and if he and they were not of the same blood, what right had he to suppose that a religious system adapted to him, could be appropriate to them? Of necessity, therefore, had Paul to assert, as he here does, that all men, as the children of God, are of one blood—subject to the same natural laws, answerable to the same moral responsibilities, exposed to the same spiritual dangers, to be benefited by the same methods of religious instruction. In this way he secured for himself a platform on which he could firmly stand while announcing to them the gospel of Christ—a platform which still remains available to the church in her great enterprise of bringing all nations under the obedience of the faith.

APPENDIX TO LECTURE V.

Development Theory.

It does not require an intimate acquaintance with science to enable one to estimate the logical worth of the arguments by which scientific men arrive at conclusions on the questions considered in this lecture. If it did, I should hesitate about offering any strictures upon their reasonings. But logic is the same for science as for other departments of inquiry, and a fallacy may be detected in the form of scientific reasoning by one who is obliged to take the materials of the reasoning on trust from the party who reasons. This consideration has been present with me in writing this lecture, and I would now take courage from it to offer a remark on the Development Theory, as it has been called. At the basis of this theory lies a fallacy which necessarily vitiates and nullifies the entire conclusion. Its exponents have confounded progress in a series with growth from a germ; two things as distinct in themselves as number and magnitude. It may seem incredible that men of ability should fall into a paralogism like this; but that they have done so, the following extract from one of the ablest of the advocates of the Development Theory will clearly show. "To suppose," says Mr. Darwin, "that the eye, with all its inimitable contrivances for adjusting the focus to different distances, for admitting different amounts of light, and for the correction of spherical and chromatic aberration, could have been formed by natural selection seems, I freely confess, absurd in the highest degree. Yet reason tells us that of numerous gradations from a perfect and complex eye to one very imperfect and simple, each grade, being useful to its possessor, can be shown to exist."[1] Now the argument here is, that though a perfect eye seems to indicate indubitably that it is the product of a designing mind, this conclusion is invalidated by the fact, that a *gradation* of eyes from the perfect to the imperfect is discoverable. A gradation in what? we ask; a gradation in the eyes of animals of the same species, or in the eyes of animals of different species? a gradation from a perfect human eye to an imperfect one, or from a perfect human eye to the imperfect eye of the lowest of the brute tribes? The latter is obviously that which Mr. Darwin has in view, for the former does not exist. But what has this to do with development or natural selection? Could it be shown that in the human race there is a gradation from a perfect eye to an imperfect, and that races, as they advance in culture, develope gradually the organ more and more perfectly; or could it be shown that a change of this sort has ever happened to the human race, a case of development would then be made out worth looking at. But to argue that the human eye has been gradually developed from that of the fish, because a gradation may be traced through different

[1] *Origin of Species*, p. 186.

kinds of animals, from the one to the other, is not less absurd than it would be, where a regular gradation in size may be traced from the eldest child in a family to the youngest, to maintain that, therefore, the former had been developed out of the latter. Absurd also is this talk about perfect eyes and imperfect. The eyes of one animal are as perfect as those of another, *i.e.*, equally fitted for the purposes for which they are designed, and for the place the animal has to occupy. We need not go to the human eye for evidences of design; the eye of an insect, a bird, or a fish, will serve as well. Each is, as an organ, perfect in relation to that for which it exists; and we never find it passing, by a series of changes, into something more perfect.

Mr. Darwin goes on to say, " If, further, the eye does vary ever so slightly, and the variations be inherited, which is certainly the case ; and if any variation or modification of the organ be ever useful to an animal under changing conditions of life, then the difficulty of believing that a perfect or complex eye could be formed by natural selection, though inseparable to our imagination, can hardly be considered real." To this I cannot reply, for I do not understand it. It may be at once conceded that the eyes of different men vary, and that these varieties may be inherited—that a man with black eyes, or prominent eyes, or whose sight is short, may propagate these peculiarities to his children. This, however, cannot be what Mr. Darwin refers to, for this has nothing to do with his subject. To what variations, then, does he refer. To variations which may occur in the eyes of the same animal in the course of life? But what are they? A man's eyes change, no doubt, as he grows older; the orb becomes less convex, the glance less piercing, the movement less quick; but are such changes propagated to his children, should he beget any in his old age? or in what possible sense can such changes be regarded as ministering to the uses of the man under changing circumstances? I feel myself quite thrown out here. That the author had a meaning which he sought to express by the words I have quoted, I am bound to believe; but what he meant by them, I confess myself utterly unable to make out.

VI.

St. Paul's Discourse—Consequences Flowing out of the Divine Fatherhood to the Race.

In asserting the universal fatherhood of God in relation to the human race, the apostle asserted a truth of vast importance and fruitful of consequences. Some of these consequences he himself expressly deduces in this discourse, and others of them are involved in the positions he assumes and the doctrines he announces.

I.

First of all, he reminds the Athenians that God, as the Father of all, has, in a sovereign manner, disposed of the different nations of men, and appointed to each its own place on the surface of the globe. As a father disposes of his estate to his sons, and as his simple will determines and fixes the allotment of each; so has God, in the exercise of his paternal rights, "appointed men to dwell on all the face of the earth, and hath determined the times beforehand, and the bounds of their habitation." God, the universal proprietor, has given the earth to the children of men; He has appointed them to "replenish the whole earth, and to subdue it; to have dominion over the fish of the sea, and over the fowl of the air, and over every living thing that moveth upon the earth."[1] And if it be asked, Why is this nation here or that nation there? the answer is, Not by accident or by any special original affinity between the place and the people, but simply because God so determined it, fixing the bounds of the habitation of each by His own sovereign will. And if it be still further asked, To what is to be ascribed the mutations of nations, the dying out of some peoples, or their absorption into others?

[1] Gen. i. 28.

the answer is, Not to any mere secondary causes is this to be ascribed, but to the supreme will of God, who hath determined the times as well as the bounds of the habitation of each. The apostle thus lifts up the thoughts of his hearers to the conception of a supreme world-ruler, who is at the same time the common Father of the race, by whose will the place and fate of nations are determined, and without whose appointment no nation can either rise or fall.

1. This representation of the apostle supplies to us a deeper and juster view of the philosophy of human history than philosophers and men of science usually suggest. Whilst, on the one hand, we repudiate the doctrine of separate centres of creation for the human race, and treat as a mere philosophic fantasy the doctrine of development, we are, on the other hand, taught by the apostle here to turn aside from the opinion, that all the varieties of the human race are due to mere differences of climate and outward circumstance. This is an opinion which the

labours of some of the most eminent ethnologists have been directed to establish; but, as I cannot but believe, without success. Without entering further into the subject at present, there is one fact which seems to me entirely to set aside this doctrine, and that is the fact of the *persistency* of races,—the retention, generation after generation, by whole communities of the peculiar characteristics of the variety to which they belong; and that under the most altered conditions of climate, occupation, food, and whatever else may be brought under the head of outward circumstances, by which it is supposed that varieties are produced. Look, for instance, at the Jews, living in every country in the world, and yet retaining unaltered the peculiar physiognomy and form of their race. Look at the Europeans settled in Africa, or the Africans in North America; the former retaining, from generation to generation, amongst Hottentots and Caffres, the colour and features of Europeans, the latter retaining amongst white men, and in the midst of civilization, the form and complexion of their African ancestors, though centuries may have elapsed since those from whom they have sprung were severed from the parent stock. That outward circumstances have an influence on the physical condition of nations is not to be denied, and I cannot but think there is reason for concluding that there is a certain typical form and habit of body peculiar to each country, and to which immigrants from other countries, in course of generations, tend to approximate; as witness, for instance, the gradual approximation of the New Englander from the round, soft features and fresh complexion of the Anglo-Saxon to the darker hue, as well as the harsher features, and more perpendicular face-lines of the North American Indian; but such phenomena will not suffice to establish the theory, that the great broad distinctions which mark off the so-called races of men from each other are attributable to mere outward causes.[1]

[1] The reader will find this subject very forcibly and

The apostle seems to me to say here all that can be truly said on the subject; These varieties exist because God, the supreme Father of all, has appointed these varieties to exist, has given to each its proper place on the face of the earth, and has determined a certain adaptation of the place to the people, and of the people to the place.

2. This doctrine of the apostle further enables us to read and understand aright the world's history, so far as it is exposed to our study. There are some men who see in the changes through which nations pass nothing but the results of fixed mechanical laws, operating with iron inflexibility and ruthless continuity, and reducing the phenomena of human existence here under the same scientific comprehension and the same mathematical determination as the phenomena of the heavenly bodies. Others, again, see nothing in the current of events but the result of either an ungoverned caprice or of

luminously treated by M. Roger de Balloquet, in his *Ethnogénie Gauloise*, p. 47, ff., Par. 1861.

the ordinary passions and tendencies of men, working out changes which are referable to no higher law, which bespeak no overruling power. But on neither of these hypotheses can a real philosophy of history be built. We can reach this only by keeping fast hold of the truth which the apostle here brings out, that all human operations are conducted under the superintending control of an infinitely wise and powerful Being, who, without interfering with man's free will, or interrupting any of the ordinary laws of nature, regulates all events according to the counsel of His own will, and uses all agencies as the instruments of a vast world-plan, of which He alone knows the compass and the details. On these two poles—God's sovereignty and universal providence on the one hand, and man's free will and self-conduct on the other—all true philosophy of history turns. Only by a due regard to these two can a just theory of the world be wrought out. If we view man as a mere piece of organised mechanism under the control of necessary law, we cannot bring the phenomena of his history within the range of moral science at all. If, on the other hand, we deny or overlook God's supremacy over the world, and His control of human interests and affairs, we are out upon a wide sea, across which no path is drawn, and over which no light rests. "Apart from the idea of a godhead regulating the course of human destiny," says the deep-thinking Friedrich Schlegel, "of an all-ruling providence, and the saving and redeeming power of God, the history of the world would be a labyrinth without an outlet—a confused pile of ages buried upon ages—a mighty tragedy, without a right beginning or a proper ending."[1] From so melancholy and tragical a conclusion we can escape only by steadfastly contemplating all things as working out the plan of Him who is alike wise and good, and who, having given to men the earth for their possession, has allotted to each people its proper place, and has determined the fortunes of each according to the counsel of His

[1] *Philosophy of History*, p. 391.

own will, without superseding the activity or controlling the mental freedom of any.

3. From this doctrine of the apostle, also, we may see how contrary to the primary order of the world, and the will of the great common Father of the race, are all attempts to extirpate races, or to drive people from the soil on which they and their forefathers have been reared, or to take forcible possession of countries already occupied. God, no doubt, may overrule such deeds for the ultimate furtherance of the race; but the deeds themselves are impious, and on the doer of them will rest the penalty of violated law and invaded right. Each nation, each people, each tribe holds the country it has aboriginally occupied by divine right—by the will of the common Father. And it is not for any other tribe of His children to stand forth and say, "Give place that I may dwell in thy land, and appropriate thy heritage, for I am stronger and better than thou." As little may any one people say to another, "Move hence and dwell in another place, for that will be

better for the interests of the world." In all such cases, under whatever plausible pretexts the aggressor may cover his act, it is an iniquity of which he is guilty—a wrong which he has perpetrated—an invasion which he has dared upon the arrangement of the Supreme Sovereign and Father of the race. We may rest assured, that however God may overrule such things for good, they are in themselves the objects of His stern disapproval, and that with those who perpetrate them He will surely reckon. Who can tell how many of the calamities that befal great nations,—the internal dissensions that waste their strength,—the foreign invasions that bring them down from their lofty place,—or the slow-working causes of decay that eat into the vitals of the body politic, and gradually sink it in ruins,—are just retributions for deeds of rapine and wrong perpetrated in the day of the nation's pride and strength on some weaker or some utterly defenceless people ? Do you think that the cry of the oppressed doth not enter into the ears of the Lord God of Zebaoth? Do you imagine that the Almighty Father forgets when any of His children cry to Him against the oppressor, the tyrant, or the robber?

II.

Another truth which the apostle urges upon the Athenians as a fair deduction from the fact of the divine fatherhood of the race, is *the duty binding on men to seek after God.* This he brings in as describing the purpose which God had in distributing the nations over the world, and allotting to each its place and time. "He hath determined," says he, "the times before appointed, and the bounds of their habitation, that they should seek the Lord if haply they might feel after Him, and find Him, though He be not far from any one of us." The apostle here describes men left without an oral or written revelation as making search after God; he speaks of that search as one, the result of which is highly problematical—"if haply,"[1]

[1] εἰ ἄραγε.

GOD TO BE SOUGHT AFTER. 155

if by any chance, if at all they may find Him; he describes their search as the groping of men in the dark, who try to find a thing by putting out their hands, so as, if possible, to feel it;[1] he intimates that though thus hidden from man's view, and to be found with difficulty, if at all, the object of their search is not far from every one of them, being their sustainer, protector, and father; and he declares that to leave men thus to seek after Him was the purpose which God had in view in distributing the nations over the face of the earth.[2] This last part of his statement presents a difficulty; for it is not easy to see the connection between the two parts of the assertion. Had the apostle said simply that God had laid on man the duty of searching after Him, and had left man to do that as best he could, his meaning would have been perfectly ob-

[1] ψηλαφήσειαν.
[2] ζητεῖν is here the infinitive of purpose or design; comp. Kühner *Ausführl. Grammatik*, § 637; Winer, *Gram. des N. Tlichen Sprachidioms*, § 45, 3; Green, *Grammar of the N. T. dialect*, p. 96, first edition.

vious. But what he says is that, with a view to this end, God has determined for nations the bounds and the periods of their dwelling; and before we can understand this we must answer the question, What is the bearing of the fact here stated on the end it is said to have been designed to effect? Now, in answer to this question, I know not what can be said, except that, by being thus distributed over the whole face of the globe, and by being thus placed under the constant control and superintendence of God, the nations had the entire revelation of God in nature and in providence subjected to their study, so that if the knowledge of God is by any natural means to be attained by man, the amplest opportunity of attaining it has thus been supplied to the race. If the lesson was to be learned at all, the means of learning it were furnished to the full; for the whole volume was spread open to man's study, and every line and letter that had been written there by the finger of God, man had the means of perusing; so that if he failed to acquire it the reason must be found in himself, and not in any deficiency in the materials of information. Perhaps, also, the apostle had in his mind some feeling of the contrast in this respect between the favoured nation to which he belonged and the other nations of the earth. That nation had been, as it were, shut up in a corner of the earth, while the other nations had been spread over its wide surface; and with this corresponded the forms under which God had conveyed His revelation to them respectively. As a verbal revelation could only, in the first instance, be communicated to a limited number, the Israelites, to whom were committed the oracles of God, were taken apart and secluded that they might receive them. But it was important also that the experiment should be fairly tried, how far man was able by searching to find out God from the book of nature and providence; and, as the leaves of this book cover all creation, it was fitting that the nations by whom it was to be read should be distributed over all the face of the earth and should be made the subjects of God's varying providential order.

The other parts of the apostle's statement present truths with which we are all familiar. That it is man's duty to search after God, is one of the primary truths of morals and of natural religion. As God's creature, and the object of His constant care, man owes to God reverence, submission, gratitude, and service. But this implies that man knows God, and is in a state of right relation to Him; for he cannot worship a Being of whom he is ignorant, and if his relations with God be disturbed it can only be by having these restored that he can be in a position to offer worship and service that can be acceptable. Now, in his present state, man neither knows God aright, nor are his relations with God such as they originally were, and ought ever to have been. Hence he needs to *seek after* God—not merely that he may get some just knowledge of Him, but that he may enter into right relations and true communion with Him. Sin has caused God to withdraw and hide Himself from man; and it has utterly disturbed and disarranged the happy relation in which man at first stood to God. When sin took hold on man, God no longer appeared to him to hold converse with him as a father with a child; and though God, in the infinitude of His grace, and on the ground of that propitiation which He Himself had provided, did not leave man to the full consequences of his sin, but has continued from the first to preserve and guide and in many ways to bless the race, yet man feels in his innermost core that *intimacy* between God and him no longer exists, that estrangement has taken place between them, and that ere he can fulfil the first duty of his creature being he has to search after God, if haply, amid the deep darkness which has fallen between them, he may get some assurance of His presence, some knowledge of His character and ways, and some ground on which to hope for restoration to His favour. This is the reason why man has so painfully to *search after*

God. In Eden God came forth into man's presence; and man beheld Him in His glory and His beauty; and man looked up into His face, and its light fell on him as that of a loving father; and man, with free and rejoicing heart, offered in return the homage of a loving and obedient child. But when man listened to the voice of the tempter, and rebelled against God, all this was changed; the free intercourse of heaven with earth was arrested; God retired from man's view within the clouds and darkness that encircle His throne; and, saving as God was pleased to reveal Himself to chosen individuals, and to one favoured nation,—the trustee of God's oracles for the world,—man was left to "grope after Him if haply he might find Him."

These words of the apostle very truly and graphically depict man's course in regard to this great matter. Endowed with a religious principle, men feel themselves constrained by the highest wants of their nature to seek after God; and yet, when left to their own unaided efforts, it has ever been only as one who gropes in the dark and at a peradventure, that they have pursued their search.¹ In a few rare cases the object of search seemed to be touched—not seen as in the clear light of day, or as by an illuminating torch—but imperfectly discerned by the dullest of the senses.² To a few of the higher and purer spirits, men of calm and serene thought and purged vision, there came, like angels' visits, ever and anon, brief

---

¹ How strikingly does the language of the apostle here, like so many other biblical utterances, find its echo in Homer! In the third book of the Odyssey, Peisistratus, expressing his belief that Telemachus, though young, would not neglect religious observances, says :—

καὶ τοῦτον ὀίομαι ἀθανάτοισιν
εὔχεσθαι· πάντες δὲ θεῶν χατέουσ' ἄνθρωποι.

"I think that he also prays to the immortals;
For all men crave after the gods."—ver. 47, 48.

Melanchthon was wont to cite this last as the finest line in Homer. In the poem of Aratus, from which St. Paul quotes, there is a similar sentiment (*Phaenom.* 4).

Πάντη δὲ Διὸς κεχρήμεθα πάντες.

"All, everywhere, we need Jove."

² *Tactus*, sensuum densisimus et infimus, convenienter hic dicitur de gentibus. Bengel, *Gnom.*, in loc.

and transient glimpses through the gloom, revelations of the hidden mystery, just and true thoughts of the Infinite. But for the mass of men it was a fruitless groping. They searched but they could not find. For them the darkness became ever deeper and deeper; until at length, baffled, disheartened, and weary, they were ready to carry their homage to any altar that priestcraft or superstition might erect, or at the best, to embody at once their deathless longings and their conscious impotence in an altar to "An Unknown God."[1]

To what is this melancholy failure to be traced? Not, the apostle reminded the Athenians, to want of means and materials of success. God, whom they thus haplessly groped after, was, all the while, "not far

---

[1] See this melancholy result of heathen speculation and inquiry fully and strikingly illustrated by M. De Pressensé in *The Redeemer*, p. 97, ff., of the English translation, Edin. 1864. The result to which philosophy conducted Protagoras in this quest was embodied in the confession περὶ μὲν τῶν θεῶν οὐκ ἔχω εἰδέναι οὔθ' ὡς εἰσίν, οὔθ' ὡς οὐκ εἰσίν, *concerning the gods, I have no knowledge whether they are or are not*. (Diog. Laert. ix. 51.)

from every one of them." By this the apostle does not refer to the fact of the divine omnipresence, so much as to the fact that it was not owing to any serious natural obstacle being in man's way, obstructing and hindering his approach to God, that he failed to find Him. Not only are the evidences of the divine existence and attributes presented in copious abundance on every hand; not only is the argument which deduces the existence and perfection of God from outward phenomena one of the simplest as well as the most convincing that the mind can contemplate; but the fact that man is the offspring of God, supplies to him the most natural help for realising, as well as apprehending, the truth concerning God. For, if man be God's child, he must have a natural capacity for God; however immense the distance between the father and the child, it cannot be that the child is, by his natural constitution, incapable of knowing the father, and approaching, in loving trustfulness and humble confidence, to his footstool. And though God be in Himself incomprehensible, so that we can never by any searching find Him out, or by any revelation be made to comprehend Him, yet if man, his child, was made by Him in His own image and likeness, there must be such an analogy between man and God, that man can pass from the knowledge of himself to a just and true, if far from adequate, knowledge of God.[1] There is thus a solid basis laid in the very constitution of man's nature, on which a true theology or doctrine of God may be built; and when the page of creation and providence is opened before a being so fitted and prepared to learn the lessons they so abundantly teach concerning God, it can only be through some perversity of his own mind that he fails to attain to the knowledge of God. This the apostle leaves the Athenians, whom he addressed on Mars' Hill, to infer for themselves; but he has himself expressly asserted the position in writing to the Romans. "The invisible

---

[1] Per ipsam animam meam ascendam ad Illum. Augustine, *Confess.* x. 11.

things of Him," says he, "from the creation of the world, are clearly seen, being understood by the things that are made, even His eternal power and godhead; so that they are without excuse, because that when they knew God they glorified Him not as God, neither were thankful, but became vain in their imaginations, and their foolish heart was darkened; professing themselves to be wise, they became fools."[1] As sin had seduced them from God, so it became the great obstacle to their receiving those right views of God which the phenomena around them so clearly taught. The darkness amid which they groped, and in which they were for the most part utterly bewildered and lost, was a darkness which had its source in themselves —in the selfishness, vanity, and folly of their own hearts.

It was thus that the nations were betrayed into idolatry. Nothing can be more absurd in itself, than to represent the Great Spirit under the similitude of any creature;

[1] Rom. i. 20-22.

and nothing can be more inconsistent, as the apostle here reminds the Athenians, than for those who call themselves God's offspring "to think that the godhead is like unto gold, or silver, or stone graven by art or man's device." Who of us would accept any image that human skill could produce as a fit representation of that which really constitutes us—our soul, our mind, our inner nature? And if we would not accept any such representation of our own spirit, how utterly incongruous and wrong would it be to suppose that by any such means there could be represented to us that Being who is the Father of our spirits, and Himself the pure and absolute and infinite spirit in whom we live and move and have our being? But into this absurdity and inconsistency man has suffered himself to be betrayed by sin. Not liking to retain the knowledge of God in his thoughts—refusing to render to Him, whose being and deity all nature proclaims, that homage and gratitude which is His due —yielding to vain, selfish, carnal imaginations; man plunged himself into darkness and all moral confusion, and so was led to change the glory of the incorruptible God into an image made like to corruptible man, and to try to find a representative of deity in figures of "birds and four-footed beasts, and creeping things."[1] This is the true origin of idolatry, of which men have speculated so much. It had its source in the darkness produced by sin; and that darkness prevented men from ever finding for themselves their way back to the true knowledge of God.

And this is the true source of all those wrong, deluding, and debasing views of God, by which men are still led astray, even where the light of written revelation is enjoyed. The depraved heart of man, unwilling to be subject to God's law, and unwilling to render to God that homage which is His due, desires not the knowledge of His name, has no liking for just conceptions of His nature and perfections, does not wish to be brought under the awful influence of His real power

[1] Rom. i. 23.

and godhead. Hence men close their eyes to the light, and prefer being at ease amid their delusions, to coming in contact with revelations which would make them miserable in their ungodliness. When men are the enemies of God, says St. Augustine, it is not from nature but their own vicious inclinations,[1] and the same may be said of those who prefer superstitious or carnal or presumptuous notions of Him to those just, sublime, and spiritualising views which Scripture and nature alike teach. Such men wilfully "turn the truth of God into a lie;" and as a necessary consequence, are left to all the religious and moral debasement which such falsehood naturally engenders. Their punishment is heavy because their sin is great. It is more becoming, says Tertullian, to believe any being not to be, than to think it other than it ought to be. And so of God; we dishonour Him more by thinking of Him

[1] Natura igitur non est contraria Deo, sed vitium; quia quod malum est contrarium est bono. *De Civitate Dei*, xii. 2.

falsely, than by refusing to acknowledge Him at all.[1] Would that all who shudder at the thought of Atheism were equally alive to the evil and danger of a false, imperfect, or fanciful Theism!

[1] Deus si non unus est, non est; quia dignius credimus non esse, quodcunque non ita fuerit ut esse debebit. *Cont. Marc.* i. 2.

VII.

Erroneous Representations of the Fatherhood of God.

In preceding discourses we have considered at some length the doctrine of the divine Fatherhood as taught by St. Paul to the Athenians, and we have seen how important and fruitful that doctrine is. Like many other doctrines, however, it has been misapprehended by some, or applied in such a way as to lead to a misapprehension or denial of other and no less important truths taught in Scripture. Before proceeding, therefore, to other points in the apostle's discourse, I must dwell for a little on this aspect of the subject. I shall especially advert to two great abuses, as they may be called, of this precious doctrine of the divine Fatherhood, which have of late been extensively propagated and eagerly defended in this country.

I.

The former of these consists in the setting forth of the truth of the universal Fatherhood of God, in relation to mankind, as incompatible with a *special* relation of paternity on the part of God towards individuals or classes of mankind. It being admitted that God is in an important sense the universal Father, it has been contended that this precludes the belief that He can be a Father to some in any sense in which He is not a Father to all; and in this way the whole doctrine of a special relation between God and any portion of our race is set aside, and with it all that we have been accustomed to teach and hold concerning divine sonship as a special privilege of the true people of God.

That I may do no injustice to the opinion on which I am about to animadvert, I shall quote a passage or two from a recent publication intended to set both teachers and taught right upon this point. It forms part of a series which bears the somewhat assuming title of "Tracts for Priests and People," and though devoted to another subject, touches on that of the divine Fatherhood. Speaking of his early religious education, the writer says:—"The church, I had been taught to believe, was a society of faithful men gathered out of the world, fluctuating day by day by new gains and losses, or transference from the church on earth to that in heaven. At the solemn season of conversion we *become* members of the church. Previous to that time we were out of all relation to God or to His church; *then* we are made the children of God, we are permitted and invited to call Him 'Our Father.' According to this view, the starting-point of life is a state of alienation from God. The Lord's Prayer, the parable of the Prodigal Son, and afterwards the whole of the Bible, seemed, and still seem to me, to teach precisely the opposite doctrine. We *are* God's children, members of His church, inheritors of His kingdom; and we are in this position, independently of our feelings or affections— nay, in spite of them." (Tract No. 5, p. 38.)

Now, with what the writer here says as to what he had been taught to believe before the true light dawned on him, I have no special concern at present. I shall only observe that, so far as it is an inadequate representation of the truth revealed to us in Scripture concerning man's relation to God, it is to be regretted that it should have been instilled into his youthful mind. And if what he has advanced in the passage I have cited, and throughout his tract, had been designed merely to guard his readers against those narrow views of God's relation to men, which go to represent Him otherwise than as compassionating those who have gone astray from Him, as inviting all to return to Him, as ready to listen to all who call upon Him, and as willing to receive with joy and love every prodigal who in conscious want and true penitence comes back and seeks admission into His house; I for my part would have cordially commended his essay, and thanked him for it. But he has, unfortunately, gone greatly beyond this. He has thought it needful to the vindication of the doctrine of the divine Fatherhood, to deny that men before conversion are in a state of alienation from God, and to maintain that all men are in the highest and fullest sense God's children, independently of their feelings and affections—nay, in spite of them. Language like this I cannot but regard as most dangerous, and deserving of the strongest reprobation. Taken in its obvious meaning, it declares that, though a man be full of hatred to God—though he deny the divine existence, blaspheme the divine character, exult in violating the divine law, revel in all that is low, sensual, and ungodly—he is nevertheless a child of God and an inheritor of His kingdom, in the same sense in which this is true of one who has undergone the process of conversion. That this is really the writer's meaning, other statements in his tract clearly show. Thus he distinctly denies that at conversion a man in any sense *becomes* a member of God's family; and asserts that at that crisis he simply returns to his rightful place in that family of which he has always been a member. And lest any should suppose that it is only *in a sense* that he thus asserts the divine sonship of all men without exception, and that he would be willing to admit that in a different sense only converted men are God's sons, he peremptorily says, "I am not to draw any line between man and man, and say, God is the Father of all men in *a certain sense,* but He is really only the Father of converted men." (P. 36.)

We are thus brought face to face with the assertion that there is *no special* sense in which God is the father of converted men— no special sense in which He is the father of any man, or class of men; but that the universal fatherhood of God is the only fatherhood that can be predicated of Him in relation to any of the human race.

Now one cannot help giving utterance to a feeling of surprise, that any man acquainted with books, and familiar with the usages of language, should have committed himself, as this writer has done, to a position which obliges him to maintain that words, expressive of human relations, are *always* to be understood in their primary and direct sense. On the assumption of this the main proof of his argument rests, and if this be denied, the whole falls to the ground. But this is what cannot be maintained for a moment in the face of common usage, not in books only, but in ordinary conversation. Every person knows, that besides the primary meaning of such words, they are constantly used in secondary, tropical, and analogical senses. Confining ourselves to the term "Father," do we not speak of a king being the father of his people? of a man being the father of a scheme, or of an institution? of old men as fathers of the nation? of the author as the father of his books? and even of fathering upon a man something that has proceeded from the genius or thought of another man? And when we go to the Bible, in how many senses do we find the word "Father" used in reference to men! Jubal is called the *father* of all such as handle the harp and the organ,[1] because he was the inventor of these instruments. Joseph is said to be a father to Pharaoh, because of the services he rendered to him as a counsellor and viceroy.[2] Job says: "I was a father to the poor,"[3] because he relieved and sustained them by his bounty. A prince is called the father of a country or of a town, as Salma father of Bethlehem, Hareph father of Bethgader, Shobal father of Kirjath-jearim,[4] etc., because he rules over it. The president of a school of the prophets is called the father of the young men connected with it,[5] because he is their teacher and guide. A man possessing any quality is said to be the father of that quality, as Abiathar, father of abundance; Abinadab, father of nobleness, and innumerable other proper names begin-

---

[1] Gen. iv. 20, 21.   [2] Gen. xlv. 8.   [3] Job xxix. 16.
[4] 1 Chron. ii. 51, 52.   [5] 1 Sam. x. 12; 1 Kings xiii. 11.

ning with Ab.¹ Abraham is called the father of all them that believe,² because of the ethical resemblance between him and all who believe. It is needless to multiply instances; nothing can be more certain than that the term "Father" is used to express many relations besides that of natural paternity. But this notorious fact is denied in the position virtually assumed by the writer I have quoted. His reasoning is substantially this; God is not a father in one sense to one man and in another to another, for the word father never can be used in any but one sense. Allow this, and his reasoning has some show of strength; deny this, and it utterly falls to pieces. Obviously, therefore, his position binds him to the maintenance of what cannot be maintained for a moment.

Another thing that strikes one very forcibly with reference to the passage I have

---

¹ See Kitto's *Biblical Cyclopædia*, Alexander's edition, under AB.
² Rom. iv. 11.

cited, is the extraordinary boldness with which the writer ventures flatly to contradict the plain and emphatic and repeated testimony of Scripture on the subject of which he is writing—unless, indeed, we find an explanation of this in his ignorance of what Scripture really does teach, in regard to man's relation to God. According to him, man, though in a state of rebellion against God, is still an inheritor of His kingdom; though full of enmity against God, is still one of His dear children; though living in sin and all ungodliness is not in a state of alienation from God. It may seem strange that any man accustomed to the use of words should think it necessary to maintain that alienation, enmity, banishment, are incompatible with sonship, or should imagine that he has disproved the existence of these simply by asserting that this relation still subsists. Absalom, no doubt, was the son of David to the end of his career; but he was not the less a rebel and an enemy when he took up arms against his father, drove him from his capital, and took possession of his throne. The prodigal, in the parable, continued, undoubtedly, to be the son of his father, even when he had forsaken his father's house, and was wasting his substance with riotous living; but so long as he continued this course, he was under his father's censure, his own heart was alienated from his father, and it was not till he became a penitent that return to his father's house was either desired by him or competent to him. Even so is it with man in relation to God: as God's creature, and the object of His constant care and bounty, man can never cease to be God's child; even these idolaters whom Paul addressed at Athens are recognised by Him as such; but does this render it impossible for such to rebel against God, to be at enmity with Him, to lie under His displeasure, to be exposed to the penalty He has denounced against sin, to have thereby forfeited all right to a place in His kingdom? The writer whom I have quoted answers in the negative; for he places alienation from God and the having God as our father in such antithesis to each other as to make the affirmation of the one, in all senses, and in every respect, the negation of the other. The absurdity of this needs no further illustration. But let us compare the assertions this writer has made as to the state of the unconverted, with the explicit declarations of Scripture on the same subject. Man, he says, does not need to *become* a son of God, for he is such already. But what says St. John? "As many," says he, "as received Him [Christ], to them gave He *power to become the sons of God*, even to them that believe on his name."[1] Nay, what says our Lord Himself? "Verily, verily, I say unto you, Except a man be born again, he cannot see the kingdom of God."[2] And to the same effect is the teaching of St. Paul, as for instance when he tells believers that they are the children of God by *faith in Christ Jesus,*"[3]—which would be of course impossible if in every sense they were God's

---

[1] John i. 12.   [2] John iii. 3.   [3] Gal. iii. 26.

children before they believed, and if all men are God's children whether they believe or not. Again, this writer asserts that *all* men are the children of God in the *same* sense. But we find our Lord and His apostles distinguishing between some whom they call children of the devil, and those whom they call sons of God;[1] how can this be if all are alike sons of God? Perhaps it may be replied, that it is possible for a man so to advance in depravity and devilishness as to lose his original dignity as a child of God, and become a child of the devil; and that it is to such that our Lord and His apostles refer. But in this case sonship is the expression of simple moral resemblance, an explanation to which the author I have quoted cannot resort without abandoning his original position; for if a man can become a child of the devil only in a *moral* sense, that is by morally resembling the wicked one, it follows not only that a man may be styled a son of God in respect of moral resemblance

---

[1] John viii. 44; Acts xiii. 10; 1 John iii. 10.

to God as well as in respect of physical relation to Him and dependance on Him, but that such *must* be taken to be the primary force of the phrase, when used of believers as in contrast with those who are described as children of the devil. In fine, this writer denies that unconverted men are alienated from God and exposed to His wrath. But what says the Scripture? "He that believeth not the son of God, shall not see life, but the wrath of God *abideth* on him. When we were *enemies* we were reconciled to God by the death of His son. And you that were sometime *alienated* and *enemies* in your mind and by wicked works yet now hath He reconciled. And you hath he quickened who were *dead* in trespasses and sins . . . and were by nature the *children of wrath even as others*."[1] Can anything be more explicit than these statements? Do they leave room for any doubt as to the condition of men, previous to conversion by faith in Jesus Christ, being one of alienation

[1] John iii. 36; Rom. v. 10; Eph. ii. 1, 3.

from and enmity against God? Do they not "emphatically convey to us the truth that the starting-point of life *is* a state of alienation from God?" And do they not, therefore, stand in direct contradiction to the positions which this writer has laid down?

I have dwelt, perhaps, on this erroneous representation of the divine fatherhood at greater length than its intrinsic importance deserves, but I have done so because of the boldness with which it has been advocated and the degree of acceptance which, I understand, it has met in several quarters. I turn now to the other erroneous representation on which I proposed to make some strictures.

II.

This consists in so presenting the doctrine of the fatherhood of God as to cast into the shade other aspects of the divine character, and especially that under which God has revealed Himself to us as a ruler and judge. This misrepresentation is closely connected with that we have been already considering;

indeed the two are only different aspects of the same error. Whilst the former, however, is chiefly advocated with a view of setting aside the evangelical doctrine of regeneration, the latter is principally directed to the invalidation of the fundamental doctrine of the atonement, or the expiatory and propitiatory efficacy of the work of Christ.

The doctrine of the atonement, as generally held by evangelical Christians, rests ultimately on the position that God, as a righteous ruler and just judge, cannot forgive sin except upon the ground of an adequate compensation being made to the law and government which He administers, for the sins which man has committed. Now, so long as we keep fast hold of the truth that God is a ruler and judge, and that our relation to Him is that of subjects to a ruler and a judge, we must feel ourselves confined by an irrefragable chain of reasoning to the admission of the necessity of some such compensation being made ere man's sins can be forgiven. Differences of opinion may arise as to the exact nature of the compensation required, and as to the kind and extent of our Saviour's acting on our behalf; but that action of a compensatory nature was required ere we could be saved, and that our Saviour's work on our behalf had its primary effect in this that it did render the compensation required for our acquittal, is a consequence to which all are logically shut up, who admit that God's relation to man is that of a righteous ruler and judge. To get rid of this, then, is the main aim of those to whom the doctrine of salvation by atonement is distasteful; and with this view, unwilling to commit themselves to anything like a formal denial of the rectoral and judicial claims of God, they endeavour to throw these into the shade, and so prevent their being taken into account, by bringing forward into exclusive prominence the relation of God to man as a Father. Let it be granted, they say, that man is a transgressor of God's will, and has, in consequence, incurred his displeasure; is not God, nevertheless, his father? and as there is no right-hearted parent who would not willingly and at once receive back and forgive his returning child when he acknowledged his offence and craved forgiveness, without requiring to be propitiated towards him or standing out for a compensation being rendered for his offences, shall we not say that God is equally ready to show mercy to His children, when they repent and return to Him? shall we dare to represent Him as less placable than one of His own creatures, and that so imperfect a creature as man? Thus, these reasoners do away altogether with the necessity of any atonement as the ground of a sinner's acceptance with God, and rest our salvation exclusively on the mercy and love of God as a father.

Now, were God *merely* a father, this reasoning would have force; to Him would belong the same privilege of managing the private affairs of His own house according to His own pleasure and will, which is conceded to every parent. But if God is a king and judge, as well as a father, the case becomes very different: the matter then passes out of the sphere of private and personal relations into that of public and official relations; there is no longer question merely of what it is pleasant, and kind, and loving to do; the stern question of what it is right and lawful to do claims precedence. A king and a judge is bound by the most solemn considerations to postpone the feelings of private affection to the claims of public duty. When public interests are affected, to make the claims of law give way to the claims of affection becomes worse than a weakness, it becomes a crime—a crime greater, because more widely mischievous, than that of the offender for whose sake it has been committed. At whatever cost, therefore, of personal feeling, the king who would maintain the honour of his throne must take order for the impartial administration of the law among all his subjects; and even though it should be his own son on whom he has to pronounce sentence, that sentence he must pronounce and suffer to be executed. Zaleucus the father may be wrung with pity for his sinning child; but Zaleucus the king must adjudge that the sentence which his son has incurred shall be inflicted.[1]

Are these writers, then, prepared to deny that God is a king and a judge, as well as a father? It would only be consistent in them to do so. But if they are not prepared to do this, why labour to keep these aspects of the divine character out of sight in dealing with a question on which they have a primary and necessary bearing? Is this the way to arrive at truth? Is this the way to construct a solid path by which the sinner may find access to God? Is it not rather to trifle with the most awful interests of man, and to persuade men to "go down to the grave with a lie in their right hand?"

If in this all-important matter we would

---

[1] See the admirable observations in application of the case of Zaleucus to the question of the Atonement in Erskine's *Remarks on the Internal Evidences for the Truth of Revealed Religion*, p. 67, 4th edit.

proceed on solid grounds, we must make our induction from *all* the facts which God has made known to us concerning Himself and our relation to Him. We must neither sink the father in the ruler, nor the ruler in the father. We must remember that if we are God's children we are not less God's subjects; if we are the objects of His affection, we are no less the subjects of His law. We must bear in mind that the pardon of sin is a question of righteousness as well as a question of mercy; and that as, on the one hand, it is impossible for God to show mercy at the expense of righteousness, it is, on the other, impossible for man really to accept a salvation which his conscience tells him has come to him through any other than a righteous channel. It is not man's heart alone that needs to be reconciled to God; it is his moral nature as well; and as conscience, after all, is the mightiest power in man, he can never be really won by any process which his conscience tells him is wrong, or dishonouring to the great moral law on which the order, and harmony, and felicity of the intelligent universe rest. When we have allowed full consideration to all the elements of the question, both as respects the revealed character of God in relation to man, and as respects that moral constitution which God has given to man, and has adapted to those relations in which man stands to Him, we shall be in the way of arriving at a safe conclusion on this momentous subject.

III.

I shall have occasion, in a subsequent discourse, to bring forward the teaching of Scripture concerning God as a judge and ruler; in the meantime let us endeavour to trace out, by the light which Scripture supplies, the whole subject of the divine fatherhood in relation to men. Now, it is unnecessary that I should go over what we have already considered as to the recognition which the Bible gives to the position asserted by the apostle in his address to the Athenians, that in virtue of our natural relationship to God, and our dependence upon Him, all men are His offspring, and He is the universal Father of the race. Assuming this as sufficiently ascertained, let me direct attention to the instances which Scripture brings before us of a *special* relation in this respect between God and certain portions of the human family. These are two:—His relation to the ancient Israel, and His relation to those who believe in the Lord Jesus Christ.

1. God is frequently in Scripture spoken of as the Father of the nation of Israel, and they as His sons.[1] Now this has respect to the fact that He was the author to them, as a nation, of special privileges and blessings. He had chosen them for Himself; He had formed them into a people; He had provided for them regulative institutions by which their national integrity was to be preserved, and their prosperity secured; He had been the watchful guardian of their national

[1] 1 Chron. xxix. 10 ; Is. lxiii. 16 ; Jer. xxxi. 9 ; Mal. i. 6 ; Hos. ii. 1 ; etc.

privileges, and had protected them amidst innumerable sources of danger and calamity. As He is the father of the race in virtue of being their creator and preserver, so was He in a peculiar sense a father to Israel, on the ground that He was the author of their national existence and the upholder of their state, who could say to them, "Thus saith the Lord that created thee, O Jacob, and He that formed thee, O Israel."[1] Indebted to Him for their selection, for their national constitution, for the entire fabric of their body politic, and for the life by which it was sustained, they could in a *special* sense claim Him as their father, and say to Him, "O Lord, Thou art our father; we are the clay and Thou art the potter, and we all are the work of Thy hands."[2]

2. This special sonship of the national Israel was typical of the still more special relation in which the spiritual Israel—they that believe in the Lord Jesus Christ—stand to God as His children. As He chose the

[1] Is. xliii. 1.   [2] Is. lxiv. 8.

national Israel from amongst the nations to be a special people unto Himself,[1] so hath He chosen saved sinners from the mass of humanity, "having predestinated them unto the adoption of children through Christ Jesus to Himself, according to the good pleasure of His will."[2] Hence believers are called, as was ancient Israel, "a chosen generation, a royal priesthood, a holy nation, a peculiar (*i.e.*, specially appropriated[3]) people." And as He formed Israel into a corporate institution, and gave them laws and ordinances for their guidance, and watched over them with fatherly care; so has He formed believers in Christ into a spiritual body, of which His son is the living head; and this He has placed under laws and rule, and constituted into a kingdom, over which He watches with peculiar care, and to the interests of which He makes all things co-operate.[4] This is the last and the loftiest of His relations to

---

[1] Deut. vii. 6.   [2] Eph. i. 5.
[3] λαὸς εἰς περιποίησιν, 1 Pet. ii. 9.
[4] Rom. viii. 28; Eph. i. 22, 23.

man; and in respect of this He, in the highest and most impressive sense, calls Himself Our Father.

This special relationship of the believer to God rests entirely on the mediatorial work of Jesus Christ. Not only has He revealed to us this new and highest view of God; not only has He been the first to offer men this high privilege, and invite them to accept it without limitation to nation or person; not only has He taught men the way to God as their spiritual father, and attracted them to God by His own example: All this is true, but it is not the whole truth, nor the part of it which, in the first instance at least, man most needs to learn. Over and above all this, the Bible teaches us that it is *in* Christ that men become sons of God—*in* Him as their propitiatory sacrifice—*in* Him as their High Priest, by whom they are brought to the father—*in* Him as their surety in whom they are accepted by God. As to this, the Scripture leaves no room for doubt. It is to those who receive Him and believe in His name that the privilege is given of becoming sons of God. Christians become the sons of God by faith in Christ Jesus, in whom they are chosen and created anew unto good works, regenerated, and so born of God. Through Him we have access by one spirit unto the father. He is the way, the truth, and the life; no man cometh unto the Father but by Him.

The relationship into which believers are thus brought, through Christ, is a *real sonship*. They are not merely, in a figurative sense, God's children; nor is it merely by a process of adoption that they enter His family; they become His sons by being created anew in His image, regenerated and born of God. The believer is thus a child of God by a process analagous to that by which man at first became God's child—a process of creation. And being thus really made a child of God he experiences all the benefits of God's special fatherly regard for him. Over all such God watches with a true paternal affection and care:—ordering all their ways in infinite wisdom, providing for all their wants with unceasing tenderness, comforting them in all their sorrows, counselling them in every perplexity, defending them from all their enemies, training them and disciplining them for a higher state of being, transforming them from the image of the earthly into the image of the heavenly, and by all His dealings with them, preparing them for that which is to be the crown and consummation of their sonship, the redemption of the body, and the glorious manifestation of the sons of God.[1] Then shall they appear with Christ in that glory which the father hath given Him, and of which they shall be made partakers.[2] Then shall the grand purpose of God be completed when they whom He hath predestinated to be conformed to the image of His son shall stand by the side of the Saviour in His kingdom, joint-heirs with Him of the heavenly inheritance, and in all respects made like Him, so

---

[1] Rom. viii. 19, 23.
[2] Col. iii. 4 ; 1 Pet. iv. 13.

that He shall appear as "the first-born among many brethren."[1]

Such is a sketch of what Scripture teaches concerning the Fatherhood of God under its various aspects. Instead of limiting that representation to man's natural relation to God as his creator, it gives great prominence to other and more special relations—relations of grace and privilege not enjoyed by all, but in virtue of which God is to some of the human race a father, in a sense in which He is not a father to all. This is the plain, unmistakable teaching of Scripture; and we do but shut ourselves out from all the benefit of this part of revelation if we overlook or deny it.

[1] Rom. viii. 29.

VIII.

St. Paul's Discourse—God a King and Judge as well as Father.

In the view which I have endeavoured to give, in these discourses, of the Fatherhood of God, my aim has been to pursue a middle course, between two extremes of opinion, neither of which seems to me to be in accordance with the teaching of Scripture. The one of these goes to deny the existence of *any* fatherly relation on the part of God towards the race as such; the other so exaggerates God's fatherly relation to the race as to throw into the shade and practically to deny His special relation to redeemed men, and also His relation to all men as ruler and judge. According to the former of these views, God, as the creator of men, comes into no other relation to them than that of ruler; they have no claim upon Him for anything but what simple justice prescribes; He is in no sense their father, who is to deal with them on grounds of love and tenderness. Now, such a view I cannot but regard as contrary both to reason and Scripture. The creation of man was a free and sovereign act on the part of God; but having been pleased to put forth that act, God bound Himself to fulfil to man all the relations naturally arising out of the nature and constitution He had of His sovereign will given to man. Is, then, filial affection to God, is love to Him, trust in Him, joy in Him, loving obedience to Him, a part of man's original constitution? Who can doubt this? Who can doubt that Adam was made capable of loving God as a father—that to regard Him with a child's trust and affection was part of the primary constitution of his nature—and that during his unfallen state he did recognise God as his father? But if Adam was thus, in virtue of his creation, made capable of sonship, and endowed with feelings which made it natural for him to love God as a father, then unquestionably the fatherly relation of God to man flows out of, and is necessitated by, the act of creation. To suppose otherwise, would be to suppose that God gave man capacities and affections for which there was no object; that as all divine endowments impose corresponding duties, that God laid upon man obligations which there were no means of his discharging; and, as a consequence of this, that the natural man is not blameworthy for acting an unfilial part towards God, inasmuch as to act as God's child is no part of his nature. Besides, on this hypothesis, what are we to make of the apostle's reasoning in his address to the Athenians? Not only does he adopt the utterance of the Greek poet, that men are God's offspring; not only does he show the grounds of that belief lying in the natural relations of men to God; but he makes it the basis of his argument against the idolatry in which his hearers were indulging. "Forasmuch then," says he, "as we are the offspring of God, we ought not to think that the Godhead is like unto gold, or silver, or stone graven by art and man's device." Obviously the apostle here assumes the fact of man's natural affiliation to God as one of the premises of his reasoning; and his reasoning is valid only on the supposition that that assumed position is true. Shall we say, then, that the apostle reasoned unsoundly here? or shall we suspect him of adopting a position which he knew to be untrue, merely for the sake of gaining an apparent advantage over those he was addressing? Neither of these suppositions can we for a moment entertain; and consequently, we must regard the apostle as here affirming what he believed to be true, what he knew to be true, when he affirmed the filial relation of man, as man, to God. And is not this what Scripture elsewhere teaches? In what sense is God "the father of spirits"[1] except in the sense that His rational creatures derive their intelli-

---

[1] Heb. xii. 9.

gent natures from Him? In what sense is Adam called the son of God[1] except in the sense that he came immediately from God's creating hand? Is it not in the same sense that angels are called "sons of God?"[2] And do we not find the prophet Malachi saying, "Have we not all one father? Hath not one God created us?"[3]—where the universal fatherhood of God is placed in parallelism with His being the creator of all, the former being involved in the latter? Surely, therefore, we may hold it as a doctrine of Scripture that God, as the creator and preserver of all men, is also the father of all? And if we are met with the objection that on this ground He may also be called the father of the devil and his angels, we need not be discomposed by it, inasmuch as we find an inspired writer not shrinking from saying that "when the sons of God came to present themselves before the Lord, Satan came also among them,"[4] a statement which, whatever

---

[1] Luke iii. 38.   [2] Job i. 6; ii. 1; xxxviii. 7.
[3] Mal. ii. 10.   [4] Job i. 6.

else it may mean, undoubtedly teaches us that there is a sense in which Satan may be ranked among the sons of God. A fallen, rebellious, doomed outcast he is, but still, as respects his original relation to his creator, one of the sons of God.

The other extreme view is the much more pernicious of the two. By sinking the character and relations of God as king and judge in those of father; or what comes practically to the same thing, so exclusively presenting the fatherly relation of God to men as to create the impression that He stands to them in no other relation, the advocates of this view sap the foundations of the entire Christian system, as a scheme of redemption, or salvation on the ground of atonement. If God is merely a father, there can be nothing properly rectoral in his administration; He cannot, correctly speaking, have His intelligent creatures under law; there can be no such thing as penalty, or trial, or judgment, in His domain. He may express His will as a father does to his children; He may chastise those who do not fulfil His will for the sake of their improvement; and He may, for their higher development and attainment, subject them to varied discipline; but a dispensation of law, sanctioned and enforced by penalties, and exposing the transgressor to judicial trial and condemnation, is wholly foreign to the idea of a fatherly system. A father may preside over an economy or house-rule; but as a father he cannot be the head of a polity or state-rule.[1] According to this theory, then, man may be an erring, and unhappy, and blameworthy child of God, but he cannot be regarded and treated as a rebel, as a criminal, as under condemnation. In this case, what need of an atonement? what need of any *remedial* scheme whatever? The father is free, surely, to forgive his own child, if he pleases to do so, without any satisfaction being rendered on the part of the child; and that it is God's pleasure to receive back and forgive every child that has

[1] Aristotle, *Polit.* i. 1.

wandered from Him, if he will but seek His forgiveness, who can doubt? Thus the doctrine of atonement is adroitly got rid of as a superfluity, if it be not denounced as a sort of blasphemy derogatory to the character and claims of the God of love; and Christianity is reduced to a mere system of natural religion, without distinctive peculiarity, and in no wise specially fitted to command the confidence, or satisfy the wants of men.

Avoiding both these extreme views, we regard the fatherhood of God as having both a *general* and a *special* aspect, the former as flowing out of His relation as the creator and preserver of man, and so extending to all men, as His creatures and the objects of His care, who "live, and move, and breathe in Him;" the latter arising out of gracious arrangements into which He enters with individuals or classes of the human race, and resting on certain special bases and conditions, and contemplating certain special results. God, as man's creator, becomes, w conceive, by that very act, both man's father and man's king—the one as necessarily as the other. And out of this double relation flows naturally the whole course of God's dealing with our race. God, as man's Father, has surrounded him with the bounties of creation far beyond what mere equity requires: God, as man's King, has placed man under law, with the strong injunction, "Do this, and live." And since man has sinned and fallen, God, as his Father, still pities him, has compassion on him, desires his return; but God, as his King, demands that satisfaction shall be rendered to His government and law ere man's sin can be remitted and the sinner can be restored. I do not see how we can lose sight of either of these views of the divine character, without injury to our conceptions of God's truth as revealed to us in His Word. If God were not both a father and a king to men, the Christian system could not have existed. It is because God is a king that a remedial system was required; it is because God is a father that a remedial system has been provided. It is the king who says, "The soul that sinneth it shall die."¹ It is the father who interposes and says, "Deliver from going down to the pit, for I have found a ransom."² God the king has denounced wrath to the uttermost against the workers of iniquity;³ God the father hath "so loved the world, that He gave His only begotten Son, that whosoever believeth in Him might not perish but might have everlasting life."⁴

With the view thus presented, the apostle's teaching in this address to the Athenians is in full accordance. Having asserted and pressed on the attention of his audience God's claims as a Father, he goes on to speak to them of how God has dealt with them as a King.

This aspect of the divine character and relation is not brought forward by the apostle in the same formal manner as the

---

¹ Ezek. xviii. 4.   ² Job xxxiii. 24.   ³ Prov. x. 29; xxi. 15.
⁴ John iii. 16.   See Appendix to this Lecture.

former, nor does he dwell on it at such length. The reason of this is obvious: his hearers did not so much *need* this part of his doctrine as they did the other. The heathen, though they had lost sight very much of God as a father, were deeply impressed with the conviction that He is a king. They believed in a divine government, of which they were the subjects; and, conscious of sin and guilt, they only too exclusively realised the fact that they were exposed to the divine wrath. By their own confession theirs was a religion of fear. Fear, says one of themselves, made the gods. Their entire service was an attempt at propitiation; to placate the gods being the prime end of all their religious actings. Of God's kingly and judicial relation to men the apostle did not need to remind these Athenians; their countless altars, their costly sacrifices, their splendid worship, their temples and statues, all confessed it; nay, the apostle had already recognised their submission to this truth when he charged them with being god-fearing overmuch. To such an audience, therefore, it was of less importance to assert the general truth of God's kingship, than to call attention to some of its practical workings in their bearing on those whom he was addressing. Assuming, then, that they knew and recognised the fact of divine government, the apostle proceeds at once to open to their minds those views of God's governmental dealings with mankind which were especially connected with the message of which he was a bearer to the nations.

In the statement with which he introduces this part of his address, it would seem as if the apostle intended to anticipate and remove an objection which might arise in the minds of his hearers in reference to what he had already concluded. "If," they might have said, "it be so wrong and inconsistent and God-dishonouring to represent the deity by images and pictures, why has this iniquity been so long endured? why has not that God, whom you say we have so grossly misrepresented and insulted, vindicated His own rights, by inflicting condign punishment on the workers of such iniquity?" This possible objection, which, it will be observed, involves the assumption of the divine rule and judicial power, St. Paul virtually meets by the words, "And the times of this ignorance God winked at;" whilst he at the same time makes this a point of transition, whence he advances to the announcement of his special message as an apostle of Jesus Christ, a preacher of the doctrine of repentance, and the herald of a judgment to come.

For the world at large, the times before the advent of Christ were, the apostle says, "times of ignorance."[1] By "ignorance" here he obviously does not mean ignorance absolutely—ignorance of everything; for many heathen nations, though utterly destitute of any direct revelation from heaven, both before Christ and since, have advanced

[1] χρόνοι τῆς ἀγνοίας. So the Arabs denote the period before the appearance of Mohammed. See Pococke's notes to Abul Faraji's *Specimen Historiæ Arabum*, p. 82.

far in the acquisition of knowledge. A flood of light had spread over many parts of the world, and nowhere more brilliantly than in the place where St. Paul uttered this discourse, long before the occurrence of that event which he regarded as the turning-point between the former times of ignorance and the latter times of which he was the herald. Of this he was well aware, and if we would understand aright his words, we must understand them on this presumption.

The ignorance of which he speaks is obviously limited and specified by the subject of which he has been discoursing—the subject of religious belief and worship. He is addressing idolaters on the sin and folly of idolatry; on the absurdity of supposing that He who made all things could be worshipped with mere outward gifts and offerings, as if He needed aught at the hand of His creature, and on the utter incongruity of acknowledging, on the one hand, the divine paternity, and on the other, representing the being whom they thus called their father and preserver by pieces of gold, or silver, or stone "graven by art and man's device." This is what he has been speaking about: it is this sort of thing which he calls "ignorance;" and the period of the world's history when this sort of thing prevailed almost universally is what he designates the 'times of ignorance."

Now, there is a danger of the term "ignorance" misleading us here, because we so often include under it, or associate with it, the idea of helplessness, inability to know, want of the means of information, that we may come to the conclusion that Paul had no censure to pronounce upon the idolatry of the Athenians and other heathen, in these by-gone times, of which he speaks. Let it be observed, then, that in using the term "ignorance," the apostle does not necessarily intend to convey the idea of *innocent or helpless ignorance.* All ignorance is not excusable. If a man *might* have known better, he is chargeable with sin, and is under blame for his ignorance. So far as this word goes, then, it proves nothing as to the light in which Paul viewed the moral character of that state of unacquaintedness with God, and his service with which he charges mankind at large. But from the whole strain of his remarks we can easily gather that he held their ignorance to be *culpable*. He plainly tells the Athenians that they *ought* to have known better; that reason and common sense forbade the conclusions to which they had come, and the practices they followed in reference to the service of God; and that, consequently, they stood condemned for their conduct. They were ignorant of God and of His worship, but it was because they had neglected or misused the proper sources of knowledge on these points which were within their reach, not because they might not have known better if they would.

These "times of ignorance," therefore, were really also times of rebellion and apostacy. In spite of the lessons of nature proclaiming on every side the being and perfections of her Maker and Lord; in opposition to reason asserting the unity, the spirituality and infinitude of God, the men of these times were idolaters, and "turned the glory of God into a lie." And as it was their heart and not their head that was at fault in this matter--as they were ignorant idolaters, because they preferred ignorance to knowledge, and darkness to light—God was pleased to leave them to the consequences of such guidance. He allowed them to go on in their evil way until they had filled the world with idols; until all sense of spiritual religion had passed from the minds of the people; until, loosened from the restraint which the belief in a personal, just, and holy God imposes, they ran wild into all excess of riot; and until, "wearied in the greatness of their way," their superstition and impurity rose to a frantic height, and all things human and divine seemed to be mingled in one mass of confusion and pollution.

So much was this the case at Athens at the time that Paul visited it, that we may well believe that many, at least, of his audience felt in their own hearts a witness for the truth of what he asserted, and were ready to admit that, with all their literature, and all their philosophy, and all their art, and their countless multitude of gods, and their splendid apparatus of worship, they had, up to the moment of his speaking to them, been immersed in the gross darkness of "times of ignorance."

Of these times of ignorance the apostle says that God "winked at" them. This is a somewhat strange, almost startling expression: what does the apostle intend to convey by it?

The original word here used[1] signifies "to look over," and may be taken either in a good sense or a bad. In a *bad* sense it signifies to *neglect something* which should have been attended to—to overlook through carelessness or indifference what ought to

---

[1] ὑπεριδεῖν, "frequens verbum apud LXX. interpretes de re quae non curatur, et sine ope propitia vel sine animadversione severa relinquitur."—Bengel.

have been observed and guarded against, and hence to contemn or despise. In a *good* sense it signifies *to pass over, through leniency or tenderness,* some fault—to allow something to go on which might have been hindered—to act, in short, *as if* it had been overlooked, though in reality it had been noticed, and was permitted only for some reason in the mind of the party who might have hindered it had he willed. Now, it is clearly in the latter of these senses that the word is here used in reference to God. Strictly speaking, He overlooks nothing, for all things are open to His sight; and these times of ignorance He had attentively surveyed from their earliest twilight on through all the advancing stages of their deepening night. It can never be said of Him that He is careless or remiss, or that He neglects anything that ought to be attended to. Were this to happen in one instance, or for one moment, the whole order of nature would be disturbed, and the machinery of being would be thrown into confusion. Still less can it be said that He in the remotest degree connived at this evil, for He is the Holy one, in whose sight all evil is unspeakably abominable, and who will not pass by sin. But God may permit sin though He does not connive at it. He may forbear to smite the sinner, though he does not overlook his sin. He may allow sin to go on uninterrupted and unchecked, though all the while He sees it in its exceeding evil, and has the means of arresting and preventing it. All this God may do; and this we take it is what St. Paul here says He did do in reference to these "times of ignorance." He permitted them. He suffered the ignorance to begin, and He suffered it to grow. He did not interfere to annihilate it by His judgments. He did not interfere to arrest it by His grace. He simply left it alone for a season; and thus left, it waxed in enormity and extent until God's purpose in permitting it was answered, and then He interposed to deal with it after another fashion.

I believe this is the true explanation of

the apostle's words, and that this is all we can say of such matters. Some there are who claim to ask more than this—who, besides knowing the fact, would know also the reason for it. But all such inquiries are presumptuous and absurd. In nature and in religion, all that we can know is the fact and order of God's acting; unless He Himself tells us we never can discover the reason of His acting. That He ever *has* a reason for all that He does, we must firmly hold; but what that reason in every case is we can no more discover, without a revelation, than we can fathom the infinite depths of the eternal mind.

There have been also persons who have made this fact a ground of argument against the divine origin of the religion of the Bible. If, say they, the Scriptures contain a religion from God—a religion such alone as He will recognise and approve, and, therefore, the only true religion for man—why was not this made universal from the first? Why were so many nations left to spend a protracted period of ignorance before God empowered those who knew this religion to announce it to the world? And having asked these questions they straightway draw the conclusion that Christianity is not from God. Now, on this it may be observed, that whether we can assign any sufficient reason or not for the late appearance of the Gospel, the argument raised on the alleged *absence* of any reason for this, is altogether futile. It proceeds upon the assumption that because no reason for it is apparent to us, there *could* be no reason for it apparent to God. But who has a right to make any such assumption? Who has a right to say: "I do not see why God, if He had this religion to send to earth, should not have sent it earlier and universally; and, therefore, I infer that God Himself could not see why this should be done; and hence I conclude that He never sent this religion at all." Surely nothing can be more unphilosophical than this, nothing more opposed to the whole analogy of nature than this;—*unphilosophi-*

cal because it builds an argument on an assumption which no man is entitled to make, and which is manifestly absurd; *and contrary to the analogy of nature,* for on every side of us we see that the creator has conferred benefits on one which He has withheld from others.

Whilst, then, we avow our inability to point out the reasons why God permitted these "times of ignorance," we feel no incompatibility between this and a cordial reception of the religion He did in due time send to remove this ignorance, and teach man the way of life. At the same time it may be observed that many important ends are manifest even to us as secured by this delay in introducing the Christian dispensation. It afforded an experimental proof of the utter inability of philosophy or human reason, without a revelation, to find out God, and to construct a satisfying religion for man. It showed also how apt man is to put away from him the truths of religion, and how, without a written revelation, these would utterly perish from the earth; for it should not be forgotten that the religion of God *was* at first universal—was revealed to the *whole* human family; and that it ceased to be universally known only because men did not *like* to retain the knowledge of it in their thoughts. And it gave scope also for that wonderful preparation of the world for the reception of this world-faith which existed at the time Christianity was introduced; as well as for the important purposes to be served by the selection and seclusion, and training and treatment of the Jewish people. That these were the reasons of the divine procedure in this matter it would be presumptuous to assert; but as these ends were manifestly answered thereby, and as great advantage was thus gained for the race, it behoves us gratefully to mark and acknowledge this, instead of foolishly and impiously replying against God.

APPENDIX TO LECTURE VIII.

DOES THE FATHERLY RELATION OF GOD INCLUDE HIS RECTORAL AND JUDICIAL RELATIONS?

THERE is a class of theologians who think something important is gained by extending the fatherly relation of God so as to *include* His rectoral and judicial relations. They admit that God is the moral governor of the universe, that He rules His intelligent creatures by law sanctioned by penalties, and that He can remit sins only on the ground of satisfaction being rendered to the justice which sin has offended; but they contend that all this falls under His fatherly relation and is the proper acting of a father.

Now, I cannot help thinking that with the men of this school it is hardly worth while to argue. They admit ostensibly all that we contend for, except our phraseology. This phraseology we borrow from Scripture, and we think it wise to retain it, because it tends to precision of thought and accuracy of representation, inasmuch as it assigns different names to really different objects of thought; but if our brethren prefer calling God a father only, to calling Him father, and king, and judge, we do not think it needful to enter into controversy with them for this, so long as they ascribe to God the functions of a king and judge as well as the functions of a father. At the same time I must add, that it seems to me not worthy of men of their character and abilities, to make a point of a matter of this sort. To say that God rules, and yet object to our speaking of God as a ruler; to say that God judges but must not be represented as a judge, is really to turn the whole question into as idle a logomachy as ever employed the pen of theologian. Supposing the point conceded, what advantage is gained by it? Is the love of God in sending His Son to redeem man made thereby more conspicuous? Is the plan of redemption rendered thereby more glorious in the view of men? Is the obligation of men to avail themselves of the salvation thus provided made thereby more imperative? And if nothing is to be gained by it to our theology, is it worth while to introduce such a departure from the time-honoured phraseology of the church, and to contend for it as if it involved some important truth? On the other hand, is there no danger to the Christian cause from this piece of neology? May not some be induced by it to forget that "God is angry with the wicked," that He will not hold the sinner guiltless, and that He will one day judge the world in righteousness? May it not encourage many to adopt a theology such as that which Shakespeare puts into the mouth of one of his characters—

> Is't enough I'm sorry!
> So children temporal fathers do appease;
> Gods are more full of mercy. Must I repent?
> *Cymbeline*, Act v. Scene 3.

And may it not be found convenient for some who with the false and shallow liberalism but too prevalent in the present day, would fain serve two masters—would like to believe with one party and speak with another—would, from regard to their own spiritual interests, hold with the universal church, and yet find themselves free to fraternize with teachers who, whatever their genius and goodness, have certainly departed very far from that "form of sound words" into the mould of which the church was first delivered. Open revolt from the truth need cause no serious alarm, for one knows how to deal with it; but the "spargere ambiguas voces" is as mischievous to the Christian cause as it is dangerous to the safety of a commonwealth.

IX.

St. Paul's Discourse.—God's Summons of all Men to Repent—The Final Judgment.

Sovereignty of power in a ruler does not necessarily involve equity of administration; and, on the other hand, a ruler may be just in principle and desirous of acting towards his subjects with perfect equity, and yet not be able, from want of absolute sovereignty, to do them all the good he desires. The union of these two constitutes a perfect reign; and such is the reign of God the King of the whole earth.

Sovereignty is the right and power of acting according to will—of giving effect to whatever the ruler pleases. Now, when this is associated with perfect equity, it can display itself only in acts of gracious benefaction. There is no other sphere left in which sovereignty in such a case can act. Equity covers the entire field of what the subject may expect of the ruler on the ground of claim or desert; beyond that lies only the province of goodness, generosity, grace—the province in which undeserved benefits may be bestowed; and this province, under a perfectly equitable administration, is the only one where sovereignty, as such, can find scope. It is not required for deeds of equity, except to execute them; it cannot, without violating equity, be put forth to injure; it can only, therefore, be exercised for good.[1]

It is in this light that the sovereignty of God must ever be regarded by us. Absolutely His sovereignty is His right and power to do what He will with His own; but, as He is perfectly just, and as justice secures that what is *due* to any of his creatures shall be bestowed, it is only in the sphere of pure benefaction, unmerited good-

[1] Williams' *Essay on Equity and Sovereignty.*

doing, that His sovereignty can be exercised. The sovereignty of God is thus practically His right and power to show grace to His creatures—to deal with them on grounds of pure spontaneous favour.

Now this gracious sovereignty God has been pleased to exercise on man's behalf in various ways. Confining ourselves at present within the limits of St. Paul's discourse to the Athenians, we note two especial manifestations of God's sovereign grace to man. The one of these is His longsuffering forbearance of man's apostacy and rebellion during the "times of ignorance;" the other is His command now issued to men everywhere to repent. That God should have permitted the idolatries and manifold sins of the heathen so long—that He should have forborne to smite those nations whose whole course was one of rebellion against Him, and whose very religion was a daily insult to Him—that He should have seemed to "wink at" their iniquities, and even continue to bestow upon them benefits innumerable, can be ascribed only to His free, spontaneous, sovereign beneficence; and to this also and not less are we to ascribe it, that for such transgressors there has been provided a place of repentance, and that God should now command all men everywhere to repent. That this should come forth in the shape of a *command* is because His grace is the grace of a sovereign; that it should have come forth at all is because His sovereignty is a sovereignty of grace.

By "the times of this ignorance" the apostle intends, as we have seen, the period in the history of the heathen world anterior to the advent of Christ. In contrast with this, he says that *now*, *i.e.*, since Christ has come, under the new dispensation, He commands all men everywhere to repent. In these words we have two characteristics of the Christian dispensation brought before us—its peculiarity as a dispensation of repentance, and its peculiarity as a dispensation of universality. In order to enforce his doctrine the apostle adds an announcement of the final judgment of the universe of men by God.

I.

Every reader of the New Testament must have noticed how prominently repentance is brought forward there as a characteristic of the new dispensation. John, the herald and forerunner of the Christ, came "preaching the baptism of repentance for the remission of sins;" the burden of his discourse was, "Repent ye, for the kingdom of God is at hand; bring forth fruits meet for repentance," *i. e.*, such as are the natural results and fitting evidences of repentance.[1] "I am come," said Jesus Himself, "to call sinners to repentance."[2] When He sent forth the twelve during His own personal ministry, they, being taught of Him, went out and preached that men should repent;[3] and when He finally sent them forth as the commissioned ambassadors of the mediatorial

---

[1] Luke iii. 38; Matt. iii. 1, 2.   [2] Matt. ix. 13.
[3] Luke vi. 12.

King, it was that "repentance and remission of sins should be preached in His name among all nations, beginning at Jerusalem."[1] In fulfilment of this commission they went forth as preachers of repentance. They began, as commanded, with their countrymen, to whom they said, "Repent and be baptised every one of you in the name of Jesus Christ for the remission of sins;"[2] and advancing from them to the heathen it was still the same message they brought; they preached to them "repentance towards God, and faith in the Lord Jesus Christ."[3] Thus they announced that "now God commandeth all men everywhere to repent." Repentance was pressed upon all men as the primary duty and characteristic privilege of the new dispensation.

The word "repent," and its cognate "repentance," are used in Scripture in two senses. In the one, they have reference to a *state of feeling*, that namely which arises in the mind when, convinced of error, mistake,

[1] Luke xxiv. 47.   [2] Acts ii. 38.   [3] Acts xx. 21.

or transgression, we are in consequence grieved and vexed with ourselves; in the other, they have respect to a *state of mind*, that namely which ensues when, convinced of error, we change our opinions, and with them our affections. The latter may be regarded as the primary meaning; for it is only as we change our views of things that we can experience a change from the love and admiration of any course, to grief and vexation with ourselves for having pursued it. To this the original word in the Greek seems to point, for that word[1] signifies

---

[1] μετάνοια, from μετανοέω, which the classical authors use as we use the phrase "to change one's mind." Thus Xenophon (*Cyrop.* i. 3), "when we had considered these things we were compelled to change our mind (ἠναγκαζόμεθα μετανοεῖν)" etc.; Plato (*Euth.* 279, c.), "having changed my mind I said (μετανοήσας εἶπον)" etc.; and Polybius uses the word very frequently in this sense; see the examples in Raphelii *Annott. in Script. Sac.*, ii. p. 726, ff. This writer also uses μετάνοια in the sense of a change of opinion or purpose; of which also Raphel gives examples. Hierocles a Neo-Platonist of the fifth century, has a remarkable passage, which may throw light on the meaning of μετάνοια, as used in the New Testament. "Since we have fallen from being good," says he, "let us endeavour

WHAT REPENTANCE IS.

literally a change of mind or opinion, and only by usage comes to include in it any reference to penitential emotion. Repentance thus viewed, therefore, is of two kinds. But practically the two cannot be separated, especially in regard to religious interests; for whenever the mind is changed in respect of religious belief and duty, there will ensue a corresponding change of feeling in respect of ourselves; our former complacency in ourselves will be disturbed, and we shall be found humbled, grieved, and vexed, because of our former errors; and, on the other hand, it is only by having our religious opinions and modes of thought entirely changed that we shall be brought out of that carnal self-complacency which reconciles us to ourselves, notwithstanding all the rebukes and

---

to regain it by a just penitence (μεταμελείᾳ) accepting the divine correction. This change of mind (μετάνοια) becomes the first principle of philosophy, the avoidance of foolish deeds and words, and the first step towards a life not to be repented of" (*Comment. in Aurea Carmina*, p. 126, ed. Needham). Comp. 2 Cor. vii. 10.

checks which conscience may address to us as sinners.

That, then, to which, under the gospel dispensation, men are called, is a change of mind and feeling. But this is a relative mode of expression, and we can understand it only by perceiving correctly, on the one hand, what the change is from, and on the other, what the change is to. *From* what and *to* what, then, are men called by the gospel to change? This question we may answer in the general, by saying that they are called to change from wrong, God-dishonouring, heart-corrupting, soul-destroying opinions, feelings, and habits, to right, true, purifying, sanctifying, ennobling opinions, feelings and habits. More particularly, the change to which the gospel calls us, is a change from wrong views of God, and wrong feelings towards Him, to such views and feelings as are right and just. Man, in his natural state, labours under wholly erroneous conceptions of God's character, perfections, and claims. He thinks of Him as a harsh and tyrannical task-master, imposing onerous duties, exacting costly services, and ready to visit with the heaviest vengeance the slightest omission of whatever He demands; or he pictures Him as an easy, benevolent, almost apathetic ruler, too indolent to notice, and too kind to punish, the transgressions of His creatures; and in accordance with the one or other of these views he either fears Him with "a fear which hath torment," or he regards Him with an indifference that borders on contempt. Among heathen nations, God is thought of as a Being who may be represented by images, who may be propitiated by offerings, and to whom the fat of sacrifices is a grateful oblation; and even where men are delivered from such gross notions, they still think unworthily of God, or they impiously turn from Him and refuse to think of Him at all. Thus is God dishonoured on the earth; thus does man become "vain in his imaginations, and his foolish heart is darkened;" and thus, turning aside from the path of truth and piety, he falls into all unrighteousness, and fills the earth with impurity, violence, and all evil.

Now, the call of Christianity to man is a call to forsake these wrong, misleading, degrading, perverting views of God, and to embrace such as are true, and pure, and ennobling. And, in order to this, Christianity presents to men the true character of God; and not only so, but presents it in such a way as to attract, whilst it enlightens. It shows to us God—the just, the holy, the sin-abhorring King, as propitiated towards us through means which He Himself, as our kind and loving Father, hath provided for us. It comes to us, at one and the same time, declaring to us the righteousness of God, and commending to us His love; it addresses the deepest convictions of our nature, whilst it appeals to the strongest emotions of our hearts; and thereby it brings us, at once in reverence and in love, to the footstool of the heavenly throne. It is this which constitutes true repentance; not mere utterances of regret, not mere bursts of sorrow, not strong expressions of self-condemnation; but the casting out of the mind of all wrong thoughts of God, and all wrong feelings towards Him, and the coming, in true child-like love and confidence, and worship, to behold His beauty, to aspire to His likeness, and to live in the joy of His favour.

It is worthy of notice how closely in the New Testament repentance is associated with remission of sins.[1] Now it cannot be intended by this to teach us that repentance *procures* remission; or that it is *on the ground* of repentance that sin is remitted. Into this opinion some have fallen, just as some have fallen into the opinion that because baptism is associated with repentance and remission, it is through means of it that the spiritual blessing is secured. But to such views Scripture, rightly interpreted, gives no support. Baptism is not the remission of sins, but simply a rite to which a person is submitted with a view to the re-

[1] Comp. Luke xxii. 47; Acts ii. 38; v. 31; etc.

mission of sins;[1] in other words, an initiatory step towards that end, and which has effect in its being a sign of submission to Christ as the teacher of that religion which makes known to men the remission of sins. In like manner repentance is not the remission of sins, nor the ground on which this is bestowed, but simply the process through which a man passes to the enjoyment of that blessing. The blessing itself comes to us on other grounds entirely; on grounds out of ourselves and independent of our working. It comes to us solely through the vicarious and propitiatory work of Christ Jesus our Lord, through whose blood alone we have the remission of sins, and by whom alone sinners can be reconciled unto God. It is only ignorance or confusion of thought that could lead any one to suppose that the mere repentance of the sinner can form a *ground* of his acceptance with God. What is there

---

[1] The preposition used in such phrases is εἰς, which "expresses a stage towards which anything advances." Winer, *Gram. d. N. T.*, § 88.

in a man's turning from a course which he ought never to have followed, to compensate to law and justice for the offences he has committed while pursuing that course? Or how could government be administered on the principle that the repentance of an offender entitles him to the pardon of his offence? If the principle be laid down that a man who violates law and incurs a penalty has only to repent to have this penalty remitted and his offence forgiven, then the legal penalty by which the law is sanctioned becomes a dead letter; for, in this case, men will be punished not for their offences but simply for their impenitence, and any man will have it in his power at once to exempt himself from the penalty he has incurred by saying he repents. If it be said that under the divine government such laxity is rendered impossible, inasmuch as not the mere saying "I repent" will suffice, but the actual repentance of the sinner as ascertained by the divine omniscience is the condition of pardon; I would ask: What does such genuine repentance imply in reference to the law? Does it not imply that the penalty denounced by that law against sin is just, and that the sinner who has incurred that penalty ought to suffer it? Suppose, then, that sincere repentance were to entitle a sinner to pardon, what would it come to? Why, to this, that when a sinner sincerely confesses that he ought to be punished, he thereby entitles himself not to be punished; in other words, that God binds himself not to do what according to His own law ought to be done, whenever the sinner sincerely acknowledges that it ought to be done! As if the sinner's acknowledgment that a certain thing ought to be done were a sufficient ground for God's determining that that thing should not be done!

From such absurdities we can escape only by holding fast by the Scripture representation, that the ground of a sinner's pardon is found in the atoning work of Christ, and in that alone; and that repentance, like faith, is simply the medium or process by

PERSONAL REPENTANCE REQUIRED.

which an individual enters into the personal enjoyment of the blessing thus provided. God bestows the remission of sins freely, without money and without price, on the ground that His kingly and judicial rights have been confirmed by the propitiation of Christ, and thereby a channel opened by which His fatherly grace may flow down on lost and perishing sinners. But in order that any man may for himself enjoy this grace, he must come unto God by a true and genuine repentance, giving up all his former wrong and dishonouring views of God; purging himself of all his former jealous, distrustful, unfilial feelings towards God; renouncing all self-righteousness in which he may formerly have trusted, and all thoughts of being able to purchase the divine favour by any works of his own; and casting himself on God's mercy for salvation as a poor, helpless transgressor, for whom there is no hope anywhere else than in the atoning death of God's own son. This is true evangelical repentance, without which there is no salvation, but in which there is no more power to procure or merit salvation, than there is power in a man to produce light by merely turning towards the sun, and opening his eyes to receive its beams.

Of this doctrine the apostle was the herald, as were all who, in obedience to the command of Christ, sought to announce to men the gospel of the kingdom. Of that kingdom, and of the dispensation with which it stands connected, this doctrine of repentance is a special characteristic. Not that there was no such thing as repentance under the preceding dispensations, or that sinners were then accepted by God on any other ground than that of the Saviour's work, or through any other medium than that of repentance and faith; but partly because this way of salvation is more clearly revealed under the Christian dispensation, and principally because the Christian dispensation, being wholly one of spiritual relations and spiritual principles, it is impossible for a man to become connected with it in any other way than through such a spiritual process as that of repentance. Under the Levitical dispensation a man became a member of the Jewish institute by birth and the outward rite of circumcision; and he could maintain his place without impeachment, simply by attending to certain outward ceremonies and observances. In such a system, as a system, there was plainly no place for an inward spiritual process like that of repentance to work. Men living under this system might be the subjects of a true spiritual repentance, and thereby connect themselves with that spiritual theocracy of which the Jewish state was the outward type; but this belonged to them as men, not as Jews, and was in no wise characteristic of the dispensation, as such, under which they lived. That dispensation was essentially outward and carnal, and its privileges were secured by purely outward processes. With Christianity it is quite otherwise. It is a dispensation of the spirit, the privileges of which are spiritual, and are to be enjoyed through spiritual processes. Hence repentance, which is a spiritual change from an ungodly to a godly state of mind, is *essential to* this dispensation—is *inseparable from* it. Unless men repent and be converted there is no entrance for them into this kingdom. A Jew was born to his place in the dispensation to which he belonged; Christians are not born but become such. The church of Christ is not a nation or visible society into which a man falls, without any choice or consent of his own, by the simple accident of birth; it is a spiritual community into which men enter of their own will, and which is kept up by continual accessions of those whom God saves by working in them to will thus to connect themselves with His church. Our Saviour said plainly to Nicodemus, "Except a man be born again he cannot see the kingdom of God;"[1] and it is this regeneration (which practically and in effect is not to be distinguished from repentance) which saves a man, and can alone

---

[1] John iii. 3

bring him to the enjoyment of the privileges of the Christian dispensation. Hence it is that repentance comes to be a special characteristic of the latter dispensation; and that the gospel of the kingdom is primarily a preaching of repentance.

II.

Christianity being thus not an outward but a spiritual system, is adapted for universality. That which is outward must be more or less local and national, but that which is spiritual is as wide as the spirit whose wants it is designed to meet. Hence, along with the fact that it is by calling men to repentance that Christianity characterisitcally pursues its end, there is the fact that this call is addressed to men universally. God "now," says the apostle, "commandeth all men everywhere to repent." Under this economy of spirituality and repentance, God addresses the world at large; His voice is to the race of men; His message is to every creature of that race; and the purport of that message is that men everywhere ought to repent, that men everywhere may repent and turn unto God.

This message God sends to men *authoritatively;* it is not left to man's option whether he will accept it or not; he is *commanded* to accept it if he would not incur a deeper condemnation and a darker doom than any to which, during " the times of ignorance," he could be exposed. This is the form in which the apostle brings the matter before his audience on Mars' hill, and it is as tending to enforce this upon them that he adds : " Because He hath appointed a day in the which He will judge the world in righteousness, by that man whom He hath ordained." The fact that there is a judgment to come, that this is to extend over all men, that it is to be conducted on the principle of righteousness, and that it is to be entrusted to one whom God has ordained, even Jesus Christ, through whom alone repentance has become possible for men, is what the apostle adduces as the supreme reason why God has so imperatively summoned all men everywhere to repent. A regard to this, consequently, must form a cogent motive to induce to repentance all to whom this message comes; and as such, doubtless, the apostle brought it before the minds of those whom on this occasion he addressed.

III.

A general belief in a future judgment seems to have pervaded all nations from the earliest times. Whether this was received at first by special revelation, as one would be led to conclude from the statement of St. Jude (ver. 14), that Enoch the seventh from Adam prophesied of this; or was a natural conclusion from the conviction that man is under a moral government here, a government by law and penal sanctions, and that as all the ends of that government are not answered in the present state, there is reason to expect a trial and a sentence in a future state ;[1] it is certain that the belief was to be found among all the ancient nations, and ever most strongly where tradition, and not speculation, determined the beliefs of men. At Athens, when Paul visited it, this belief, though sneered at and mocked by the philosophers and wits, still formed part of the popular creed. At the same time it cannot be said that it was any clear or definite or very impressive conviction which was generally entertained by the heathen on the subject; beyond a mere vague expectation of some trial which each man had to undergo after death, and certain fantastic stories which poets and mythologers had concocted about the manner and circumstances of the trial, it cannot be said that the subject had much hold on their minds. Hence what the apostle announced to the Athenians at this time would come upon them with all the force and excitement of a new truth.

And in the form in which he put it before them it *was* new. It was a new thing

[1] See Butler's *Analogy*, Part I. ch. 2.

to them to be told that the supreme God Himself was to be the judge of mankind. It was a new thing to be told that the judgment to come was to be a simultaneous as well as a universal judgment of the race. It was a new thing to be told that a day has been fixed in the councils of heaven, when this tremendous assize is to be held. And it was of course all new to them that it was in the person of Jesus Christ—of one in human nature that God was to judge the world. So utterly strange to them was all this that their patience was exhausted by the strain thus laid on their powers of belief, and they, with a few exceptions, broke away from the speaker with derision and mockery.

What the apostle told the Athenians in this discourse, is what Scripture constantly teaches us concerning the judgment to come. It assures us that the judgment will be universal and simultaneous. God will then *"judge the world."* Before His tribunal shall be summoned every son and daughter of Adam, with their progenitor at their head.

As the Judge descends to take His place upon the throne the voice of the archangel and the trump of God shall be heard, and they that are in their graves shall come forth. The long slumber of centuries shall be suddenly broken. The tombs of many generations shall be unsealed in a moment. From crowded grave-yard, and from lonely sepulchre; from battle fields, where countless hosts have fallen in one fell slaughter, and men who have died in the agony of conflict have been buried in one common grave; from the untrodden depths of ocean, which no sunbeam has ever reached, but to which the strength of manhood, and the gentleness of woman, and childhood's smiling loveliness, have gone down and returned no more; from the burning desert, where the bones of the hapless traveller have lain bleaching on the spot where he sank down and died; and from mountain cave, where the fugitive or the solitary has yielded up his spirit when there was no one by to help him;—wherever man's mortal frame has found a resting-place where it could return to its parent dust, the forms of living men shall be seen coming forth that they may stand before the Judge. It will be the closing scene of this world's history—the catastrophe of that strange drama which through the ages has been enacted on the theatre of earth; and all who have had a part in its long and eventful development shall be there to witness the solemnities of its close, and receive the award of the Judge.

This award shall be one given "in righteousness." The standard by which the Judge shall determine the case of each, will be a perfectly righteous standard; the decision of the Judge will be such as every conscience shall approve as just and right. How can it be otherwise when it is God who is the judge? "Shall not the Judge of the whole earth do that which is right?" Is it possible that any other than perfectly righteous judgment should proceed from "the righteous Lord who loveth righteousness?"

The standard of decision at that great assize shall be the moral law of the universe, under which God has placed all His intelligent creatures; and the testing question, in each case, will be: Has that law been kept as it ought to have been kept? To determine this the character and conduct of the individual, whilst on earth, will be strictly investigated; a survey of his entire existence here below will be taken; every thought, and word, and deed, of which he has been the subject whilst on earth, shall come into judgment; and from the general tenor of the whole it will be made manifest for what place and for what society he is fitted—whether for the place and society of those who love God supremely and delight to do His will, or the place and society of those whose hearts are wholly alienated from Him, and whose constant aim it is to dishonour and disobey Him. In the forming of this judgment due respect will be had to the circumstances of the individual whilst under probation—the talents he possessed, the privileges he enjoyed, the oportunities with which he was favoured. This both the reason of the case and the clear declarations of Scripture forbid us to doubt. We cannot believe it compatible with a perfectly equitable decision, that those whose lot was cast in times of ignorance or amid unfavourable circumstances should be dealt with in the same way as those who have been privileged with the light of revelation, the offers of the gospel, and the means of grace. The moral differences which exist between different persons are often very great; and in forming a judgment as to the moral worth of the conduct of each it is as needful that these differences should be taken into account as it is needful that differences of weight, and force, and motive power should be taken into account in estimating the comparative merits of machines. To man, limited in knowledge and limited in faculty, such comprehensive survey is impossible; and therefore all human judgments of the moral worth of individual agents are more or less imperfect. But to the judgment of God no such imperfection attaches. To His omniscient scrutiny all things stand revealed; and in His infinite mind every element that bears on a perfectly equitable decision in the case of each of His intelligent creatures receives due consideration. That this shall be the principle of His adjudication He Himself has assured us. To whom much is given of them the more shall be required. The servant that knew his master's will and did it not shall be beaten with many stripes, while the servant that knew it not shall be beaten with few stripes. It will be more tolerable in the day of judgment for Sodom and Gomorrha than it will be for those cities in which the Saviour preached. They that have been exalted to heaven by privilege shall, if they fail to improve them, find that that exaltation only procured for them a deeper fall and a heavier doom.[1]

From this searching scrutiny no being of our race shall come off scatheless. All

[1] Luke xii. 47, 48; Matt. x. 15; xi. 20-24.

shall be found to have transgressed the law and thereby incurred the penalty. How, then, shall any escape? The answer to this is furnished by that announcement which the apostle made in this discourse to the Athenians, that "now God commandeth all men everywhere to repent." To such as obey this command and turn unto God through that way which He has provided, salvation is sure. United by faith to the Redeemer, His righteousness is imputed to them; they are made the righteousness of God through Him; they receive the redemption of their souls, even the forgiveness of their sins; for them there is no condemnation; Jesus has delivered them from the wrath to come; and they are exempted from the doom they have merited, being accepted in the Beloved.[1] At the great trial all this will be made manifest, and their acquittal shown to be in full accordance with perfect righteousness.

[1] 2 Cor. v. 21; Col. i. 14; Rom. viii. 1; 1 Thess. i. 10; Eph. i. 6.

For this judgment a certain time is fixed; "God hath appointed a day in the which He will judge the world. The apostle here uses phraseology with which his auditors were familiar; for, "to fix a day," or " determine a day for any one," was a common expression with them to indicate the summoning of such an one to trial.[1] St. Paul thus conveyed to the Athenians the idea that the judgment of which he spoke was a settled thing. The event is certain, and the time is fixed. The judgment of the world will come, and the world has but a limited time to exist ere the day shall dawn that is to summon its intelligent tribes to the presence of the judge. Then the probation of the race shall be ended; then the issues of the countless streams of human activity that have been gliding through the ages shall be gathered up; then the sum total of the world's manifold and eventful history shall be taken;

---

[1] πᾶσι δ' ὁρισθείσης ὑπὸ κηρύγματι μιᾶς ἡμέρας εἰς κρίσιν. Appian, *B.C.* iii. p. 948. Comp. Si status condictus dies intercedit cum hoste ito. *Legg.* xii. *Tabb.*

then the mystery of God will be finished, the economy of redemption wound up, and the enigma of divine providence solved. This day shall be "the period of this earthly system, the dying day of this great world; on which its last groans will be heard, its knell sounded through the universe, and its obsequies celebrated with most awful pomp and supreme as well as melancholy grandeur."[1]

This day is fixed in the counsels of heaven. But it has not been revealed to men, and the season of its coming no one can foresee. Nor will it come after many premonitions and omens of its approach. It will come as the flood came, whilst men are eating and drinking, marrying and giving in marriage. It will come as Christ came, when the world was asleep, and darkness was around the abodes of men. It will come as a thief in the night, and the shout of the descending judge, and the pealing blast of the archangel's trump, and the

[1] Dwight, *Theology*, Serm. clxvi.

shaking to its centre of the troubled earth, and the bursting open of the graves, and the rending of the rocks, and the rushing forth from unsounded depths of those imprisoned fires which are to consume the globe and spread upwards to the arched heavens, involving all visible creation in one blazing ruin: —these shall be the first intimations to the world that its day of doom has come. With a scene like this before his prophetic view, can we wonder that our Lord should have left the injunction to his disciples in all coming time to be ready, seeing they knew neither the day nor the hour when the Son of man cometh?

And as the day is appointed, so also is the Person who is to appear and act as the judge. God will judge the world, but not immediately and in His own person. There is One whom He hath constituted judge of all; one who shares our own nature, and who, having once lived and died on this earth, has been raised from the dead that He might sustain the office and perform the functions of universal Lord and Judge. The apostle does not name Him to the Athenians, but there can be no doubt to whom he refers when he says, "that God shall judge the world by that man whom He hath ordained." The general testimony of Scripture leaves us in no doubt as to the fact that it is our Lord Jesus Christ who is to be the final judge of all. He Himself, whilst on earth, declared that the Father judgeth no man, but hath committed all judgment unto the Son; and He told those who sat in judgment on Him, when He stood arraigned at the bar of men, that they should hereafter see the Son of man sitting on the right hand of power, and coming in the clouds of heaven as the judge of all.[1] Still more explicitly and fully did He discourse to the people on this point, telling them that the Son of man should come in all His glory, and all the holy angels with him, and sit on the throne of His glory, and before Him should be gathered all nations, and He should

[1] John v. 22; Matt. xxvi. 64.

separate them one from another as a shepherd separateth the sheep from the goats; and then went on to describe to them the process of the judgment, and show them its final issue in the sending of the wicked to everlasting punishment, and the admission of the righteous to life eternal.[1] To the same effect are many statements in the writings of the apostles, which it is unnecessary to quote.[2] Nothing is more certain, concerning the final judgment, than that He who is to occupy the throne and administer the judgment is the Man Christ Jesus; who, though for a season made lower than the angels for the suffering of death, is now crowned with glory and honour, and will at the appointed time come forth as the supreme arbiter of the universe to summon the nations to His bar, and to judge every man according to the deeds done in the body.[3]

---

[1] Matt. xxv. 31-46.
[2] Comp. Rom. ii. 16; xiv. 9, 10; 2 Cor. v. 10; 1 Thess. iv. 16; Jude 14, 15.
[3] Heb. ii. 9; Matt. xxv. 32; Rev. xx. 11-15.

For this He is fitted by the glorious constitution of His person, as God no less than man. But for His essential deity He never could occupy such a post; no appointment, no decree, no exercise of power could fit Him for it. He, who is to judge the world in righteousness, *must* be divine. Omniscience and omnipotence are both required for such a task, and these belong only to God. To speak, as some have done, of delegation in such a case, as if God shall judge the world by Christ as an earthly sovereign judges by means of a substitute appointed to act in his name, is simply absurd. Omnipotence cannot be delegated; omniscience cannot be transferred. He who does a work for which these are required must be Himself divine.[1]

Such were the new and startling revelations by which the apostle sought to give weight and force to his announcement, that God now commandeth all men everywhere

---

[1] See Wardlaw, *Discourses on the Socinian Controversy*, p. 159, 4th edit. Pye Smith, *Scripture Testimony to the Messiah*, vol. ii. p. 35, ff., 4th edit.

to repent. An effect of this kind they are well fitted to produce. Nothing so brings home to the soul a sense of responsibility as the prospect of a judgment to come, a judgment in righteousness, a judgment that shall take cognizance of the entire life, and proceed to an unalterable decision upon an impartial survey of every work, with every secret thing, whether it be good or whether it be evil.[1] As soon as the belief of this takes possession of the mind, conscience becomes alive, and "the powers of the world to come" begin to cast their solemn shadows over the soul. Frivolity gives place to earnestness,—self-confidence to a poignant consciousness of deficiency, pollution, and transgression,—worldliness and carnality to a profound sense of the vanity of all present pursuits and enjoyments, in comparison with the mighty interests of that final state into which the judgment is to introduce us; and thus over the entire inner nature of the man there is brought a change, which in itself is

Eccles. xii. 14.

a part of repentance, and tends towards the consummation of that great spiritual change by which the soul is brought to God. When men are constrained to realise the fact, that the brief period of life is that which alone is given to them to prepare for a trial which is to determine their eternal condition, and when, along with this, they are brought face to face with the fact that as sinners they are liable to a sentence of condemnation when they shall stand before the judge; the easy excuses with which they are wont to palliate sin and soothe themselves into indifference are scattered to the winds, and, in all the earnestness of a soul that feels itself in peril of eternal ruin, they are impelled to cry out, "What must we do to be saved?"

The apostle sought to produce this effect on the minds of his auditory on Mars' Hill. Can it be unseasonable to remind the reader that the same considerations are fitted to produce the same effect still? Is it not worth while that he should pause and ask whether he has allowed them their due weight in his mind? Has he felt how solemn a thing it is to be living a life every part of which is telling on his eternal destiny, and for every part of which he has to give account to an omniscient judge? Does he consider, as he ought, how every day is bringing him nearer to the time when he shall have to abide that awful scrutiny? Is he prepared to meet the judge? And if he thinks he is, to what is it that he trusts for acquittal when brought under His penetrating eye, and His impartial judgment? Questions these which no wise man will put away from him, or answer carelessly or lightly!

"It is but a little ago," said Augustine, addressing a friend on this subject, "since you witnessed how, when at the shrill trumpet-peal, and the clamour of the Goths, the city of Rome, the mistress of the world, oppressed with sadness and terror, trembled. Where then was the rank of nobility? Where definite and distinct grades of dignity of any kind? All things were mingled and confused through terror, wailing in every house, equal fear pervading all. Slave and noble were as one; to all the same image of death was present, save only as those to whom life had been most joyous feared death the most. If, then, men so fear their foes and a human hand, what shall we do when the trumpet shall have begun with appalling clangour to sound from heaven, and the whole world shall re-echo the voice of the archangel louder than any trumpet's peal? when we shall see brandished over us not arms made with hands, but the very powers of heaven moved? What fear shall then seize us, what gloom, what darkness, if, often warnèd, that day should yet find us unprepared!"[1]

[1] *Ad Demetriadem, Ep.* cxlii.

X.

St. Paul's Discourse—Conclusion and Result.

The announcement of the fact of a future judgment of the whole human race, to be conducted by one in human nature, could not but startle and astonish St. Paul's hearers on Mars' Hill, accustomed, as they were, to put such considerations very much away from their minds; or, when they turned their thoughts in that direction, to form to themselves a very different conception of what lay before them in the future state. This fact, however, it was not only of importance in the general that they should be assured of, but it had such an immediate bearing on the main theme of the apostle's discourse, that he could not, in justice to his

ST. PAUL'S DESIGN.   267

subject, overlook it. He had sought to shut up his hearers to a sense of sin, in that they dishonoured God by their idolatry, and he had met a possible objection to that which their long impunity whilst living in the practice of idolatry might have suggested, by telling them that "the times of this ignorance God had winked at," whereas "now He was commanding all men everywhere to repent." To complete his position, to make it coherent, to justify it, and to send it home with due force to the minds of his hearers, there only needed such a further statement as that which he gave when he announced to them the fact of a future universal judgment in righteousness. He thus referred them for an explanation of whatever was strange and unaccountable to the human reason in God's dealings with mankind, to that time when, by His righteous decisions, He should vindicate the method of His providential rule, and "justify the ways of God to men." Within the range of that wide scrutiny "the times of ignorance" would fall, and God would then show how His winking at these was in full accordance with righteousness; whilst on the other hand, having now entered upon another method of dealing with men, and having, in pursuance of it, commanded all men everywhere to repent, the prospect of a righteous judgment, in which each man should be tried according to his privileges and opportunities, and each should receive an award exactly in accordance with what equity demands, was well fitted to enforce this command. The apostle might hope also, by giving prominence to such announcement, to produce an impression favourable to the main object of his mission as an ambassador for Christ. He might hope thereby to awaken in them a feeling of earnestness, to bring over their too frivolous minds a shadow of solemnity and anxiety, to subjugate them to "the powers of the world to come," and thereby the better induce them to give heed to what he had further to unfold to them concerning God's relations to mankind, and especially concerning that way of salvation which God has provided by the work of His Son.

That the apostle was about to open to his audience more fully and minutely the doctrine of Christ, appears evident from what is stated in the close of ver. 31. The meaning of this part of his address is somewhat obscured in our version by the use of the addition "whereof;" the statement "whereof He hath given assurance unto all men in that He hath raised Him from the dead," being apt to lead the reader to suppose that the apostle means to adduce our Lord's resurrection as affording some proof or evidence or demonstration that God will, on a certain day, judge the world in righteousness by the man whom He has appointed. It is not easy to see how this could be, for there seems no such connection between the fact of a future universal judgment by Jesus Christ and the fact of His resurrection, as that the one should give assurance or proof of the other. But this rendering does not convey the proper meaning of the apostle's words. What he intends is, that God has furnished to all men sufficient ground *for believing in Jesus*, by having raised Him from the dead; in other words, that having raised Him from the dead, God has thereby fully accredited Him to be all that He claims to be, and all that He is set forth in the message of His servants as being, so that men may on the most solid grounds have faith in Him as the future judge of all.[1]

Every reader of the Acts, and of St. Paul's epistles, must be aware how much the apostle was accustomed to rest the evidence of the doctrine he preached on the fact of the Lord's resurrection. Wherever he came he was careful to announce this as the great

---

[1] The verse literally rendered is: "Because He hath appointed a day in which He will judge the world in righteousness, by a man [or in the person of a man] whom He hath ordained, having afforded belief (*i.e.*, reason for belief) in that He hath raised Him from the dead." The phrase παρέχειν πίστιν, according to accredited usage, means *to furnish grounds for belief, to accredit, to warrant belief in*. See the copious collections of Wetstein in his note on this passage, and the illustrations of Raphel and Kypke on this place.

fact of which He was a witness; and whether to Jew or to Greek, it was of this he spoke as the grand demonstration of the claims of his master to be regarded as the Messiah, and to be reverenced as a teacher sent from God. With this he seems to have begun his ministry at Athens when he taught in the Agora; with this, we know from his own statement, he opened his commission at Corinth;[1] this he carried with him when he went up to Jerusalem; and so constantly did he put this in the very front of his testimony, that he became noted among those who were not Christians as a person who affirmed that one Jesus who was dead was alive.[2] The apostle knew well the immense importance of this fact to the religion which he taught. He felt that, with this to fall back upon, he need fear no assault that could be made upon the divinity of its origin. To him it seemed strange that any should think it incredible that God should raise the dead,[3] and being assured that Jesus Christ who had

---

[1] 1 Cor. xv. 3-8. [2] Acts xxv. 19. [3] Acts xxvi. 8.

been dead and buried had been raised again from the dead, he saw in that the operation of God, and accepted it as God's attestation of the claims and authorisation of the doctrine of Jesus. By His resurrection from the dead, Jesus, in the judgment of the apostle, was declared to be the Son of God with power,[1] that is, so as to carry irresistible conviction to the mind that He was really so. St. Paul felt strongly that if he were deprived of the support of this fact, he would be deprived of everything that was essential to him as a herald of Christianity. "If Christ be not arisen," he exclaimed, "then is our preaching vain, and your faith is also vain."[2] In this fact also he found a fruitful source of strength and establishment for those who had committed themselves to the acceptance of Christianity as a religious system; for, in the resurrection of Jesus, he recognised God's attestation of the sufficiency of that propitiatory work which the Saviour had come to accomplish, and along with that the pledge

[1] Rom. i. 4. [2] 1 Cor. xv. 14.

and assurance of the resurrection to life and glory of all who believe in Him. As He was delivered on account of our offences, so was He raised again on account of our justification; in either case a divine purpose was contemplated by the event of which He was the subject.[1] By faith in Him the soul becomes one with Him, and so we participate in His resurrection; "by baptism into death we are buried with Him;" in order that "like as Christ was raised up from the dead by the glory of the Father, even so we also should walk in newness of life." Having been quickened from the death of sin in which all men naturally are, believers in Him are raised up together, and are made to sit together in heavenly places in Christ Jesus.[2] And being thus vitally united to Him, they have a certain assurance that as He rose from the dead so shall they; for "if," says the apostle to the Romans, "the spirit of Him that raised up Jesus from the dead dwell in you, He that raised up Christ from the dead

[1] Rom. iv. 25.   [2] Rom. vi. 5.; Eph. ii. 5, 6.

shall also quicken your mortal bodies by His spirit that dwelleth in you."[1] In the resurrection of Christ, therefore, the apostle found at once the divine authentication of his mission, and the vital source of present privileges and future triumph to all that believe in Him.

Of this fact the apostle was well assured himself. Not only had he the testimony of those who had been the companions of the Lord during His earthly sojourn, and who had seen Him and conversed with Him after His resurrection, but he could himself say, "Have I not seen Jesus Christ the Lord?"[2]— that is, as the connection shows, seen Him since His resurrection so as to be a competent witness of that fact, and to receive from Him as the risen Lord commission to act as an apostle. And being well assured of the fact himself he boldly attested it wherever he went, and appealed to the unanimous consent of a multitude of competent witnesses as affording the proper kind of evidence in

[1] Rom. viii. 11.   [2] 1 Cor. ix. 1.

such a case, and as affording it in such degree as to render all scepticism on the subject unreasonable and blameworthy.

This evidence he would doubtless have submitted to the Athenians had he been permitted to finish his discourse : and he would doubtless also have unfolded to them the whole doctrine of Jesus, delivering unto them, as he did a few weeks later to the Corinthians, "that which also he had received, how that Christ died for our sins according to the Scriptures, and that He was buried, and that He rose again the third day according to the Scriptures."[1] But his audience were not inclined generally to hear any more of what he had to say to them. So long as he kept on the ground of mere natural reason they seem to have listened with patience and perhaps with interest; or it may be they bore with his discourse on these points in the expectation of having their curiosity gratified when he came to speak of those "new things" of

[1] 1 Cor. xv. 1-3.

which they supposed him to be the teacher. But when, instead of something to satisfy their curiosity and amuse their ingenuity, he brought forward what was fitted to awaken conscience, and to elevate them to the sphere of real spiritual earnestness; and when he began to touch upon points more especially belonging to the Christian revelation, they were offended, and hastily broke up the assembly: some assailing the apostle and his doctrine with mockery,[1] while others more courteous, though not less determined in their hostility, said, "We will hear thee again of this matter."[2]

---

[1] How the Athenians could rid themselves of a speaker whose sentiments they disliked, may be seen from what Plato makes Socrates say in the *Protagoras* (p. 319, c). "The Athenians," says he, "when any one would address them whom they think not competent to advise them, however respectable, wealthy, or well-born he may be, do not permit him, but laugh him down and make a tumult, until either he retire of his own accord, overcome by the uproar, or the officers carry him off."

[2] Some commentators, among the rest Calvin, Grotius, and Bengel, suppose that the proposal to hear Paul again was *sincerely* made. But if so, the apostle would hardly have left the city without making another attempt to con-

The part of Paul's discourse at which his hearers took especial offence was his reference to a resurrection from the dead. When they heard of a resurrection of dead persons [1] some mocked (*i.e.*, interrupted Paul with exclamations of ridicule), and others said, "We will hear thee again of this matter." What offended them was not, as the authorised version would lead one to suppose, the announcement by Paul of a general resurrection; for of this he had said nothing, nor is it to be supposed that these Athenians would perceive that the resurrection of all the dead is in any way involved in the resurrection of Jesus, this being a peculiarly Christian revelation which was startling and offensive even to the Jews (comp. iv. 2). What they could not bear was his announcement of such a thing as a resurrection at all—the resurrection from

vince them; a sincere offer to hear him again, on matters that were so important in his estimation, would have appeared to him in the light of an engagement which he was bound to fulfil.

[1] Ἀνάστασιν νεκρῶν, both words without the article.

the dead of even one person. Of such, in fact, they had never had experience, nor had the idea of it a place in their minds. It is to revelation alone that men are indebted for a knowledge of such a fact. Though nature offers certain analogies which tend to illustrate the belief *after* it has been created by revelation, there is nothing within the range of ordinary experience that would of itself lead to such a belief, or even suggest it to the mind. To nature, death is wholly anomalous and mysterious; and the violent disruption which it produces of the whole continuity of nature, precludes the possibility of any certain conclusions being drawn by the natural reason as to what may be the condition of the soul after death. This terrible event suffices even to shake the confidence of many in the continued existence of the soul in the separate state; what wonder, then, if it should utterly shut out of men's minds the idea of a resuscitation and rehabilitation of the body? What is there in nature to suggest the expectation that that frame which we see entirely decomposed and mingled with the common dust of earth, should once more be recomposed, and ⌣raised up and endowed with life? What is there in nature to awaken the hope that this terrible catastrophe which has shaken to utter ruin the fair fabric of man's frame is but a step towards its resuscitation in a nobler and more enduring form? Do not all the appearances which death produces fix on the mind the melancholy conclusion, that with it man's history terminates, that with it begins a night for which there is no morning? When Job, in the bitterness of his soul, exclaimed, "There is hope of a tree if it be cut down that it will sprout again, and that the tender branch thereof will not cease. . . . But man dieth and wasteth away, yea, man giveth up the ghost, and where is he?"[1] he spoke the common feeling of the race, under the mere teaching of nature. For his sad question nature has no clear and

[1] Job xiv. 7, 10.

satisfactory answer. Only an express message from heaven can tell us that the ruins of death may be repaired, and can meet us at the grave with the assurance that we shall "receive our dead again."

But though the announcement of a resurrection of one who had been dead would thus of necessity be a new and strange announcement to the Athenians, there seems no reason why it should have offended them so much as to lead to the sudden breaking up of the assembly which had hitherto been listening to the apostle. Granting that the announcement was new to them, there was nothing in that to offend them, but on the contrary, something rather fitted to attract persons devoted as they were to the gratification of curiosity; and although it would doubtless seem to them a very improbable thing which the apostle announced, yet one might imagine they would have been moved to hear all that Paul had to say about it, and to see what he would make of it for his purpose. Instead of this, however, they either rudely interrupted him with expressions of ridicule, or politely excused themselves from any further listening to him, by adjourning the conference for an indefinite period. How are we to account for this? We may account for it by supposing that it was not this announcement itself which offended them, so much as the general tenor and tendency of the apostle's discourse, especially in the latter part of it; and that they merely made the announcement of a resurrection the occasion for giving vent to feelings which had been gathering to a height as they listened to the apostle's previous words. In addition to the offence which the carnal mind receives from all that is spiritual and earnest in religion, there was something in the train of the apostle's discourse on this occasion which was fitted to give special offence to the Athenians. Their passionate love of art, and their general culture, had given a prevailing sensuous tone to their minds, had created in them a love of the outwardly beautiful and symmetrical, had led them to be averse from the contemplation of spiritual realities, and especially such as were calculated to disturb or agitate the feelings. Their life was supremely a life amid present things. They loved to surround themselves with what pleased the eye and gratified the taste. They felt that life was but brief, and that it was a pity to waste any portion of it on what did not minister to present enjoyment. Their heaven was here; their affections were rooted in the present state; their interests were bounded by "this visible diurnal sphere;" and they liked not to cast their thoughts into the gloomy void, as it seemed to them, that lay beyond. Hence, death, and a state after death, were as much as possible excluded from their thoughts. These were not subjects which it was deemed proper or courteous to obtrude upon society. This was a field where art sought not to exercise itself, or into which it entered only to throw as much as possible a graceful charm over the hated reality. "Direct representations of death," says the greatest authority on ancient art, "and the ceremonies observed thereat are rare in Greek art."[1] So rare that he has not adduced any instance that can be considered conclusive. In some of the remains of Greek art we find poetical and allusive representations of death as a departure, a going on a journey, "but without further indication of the unknown bourne whither it is directed," and some which are supposed to identify the god of death with the god of sleep. In their attempts to represent scenes of future felicity, these ancient sons of genius could rise no higher than the picture of an earthly banquet from which even its grosser peculiarities were not excluded. Everything, in short, betokens a sensuous people, who shrank from what would disturb or agitate the mind, and loved to dwell amidst pleasing images of earthly beauty and enjoyment. Now, in all ages persons of this class resent nothing so much as an attempt

---

[1] Müller, *Ancient Art and its Remains*, by Leitch, pp. 512, 509, 444.

to obtrude upon them truths connected with the spiritual and eternal world. It offends their taste; it disturbs their equanimity; it breaks up their carnal dream; it interrupts the continuity of their sensuous existence; it forces on them anticipations from which they naturally shrink; and it obliges them to realise facts they would fain forget. Hence, however gently and courteously the subject may be introduced, the very mention of it is apt to irritate them, and they either break out in anger against the person who has introduced it, or with some cold and formal courtesy they deliver themselves from his presence. So it was with these Athenians. The offence which the apostle gave them consisted chiefly in that he summoned them to look earnestly on spiritual realities, and obtruded upon them truths which awakened their dormant consciences, and brought the bright sensuous world in which alone they delighted under the shadows of the world to come.

The apostle was thus taught the painful

lesson that not Jewish prejudice alone, not barbaric ignorance alone, but the highest culture and the habits engendered by free thought and unfettered speculation as well, were at enmity with the truths which he was sent forth to preach. He had done his part nobly and fearlessly; he had confronted ethnic philosophy and religion in the very centre of their strength and influence; he had brought the truth to bear in a manner at once delicate and decided upon the minds of an audience in the metropolis of human culture and refinement; he had spoken wisely and kindly to those whom he addressed, striving to accommodate his speech to their modes of thought, giving them credit for whatever was true in their religious beliefs, and seeking from the stand-point of their own system to lead them on to higher and more spiritual views. And what had been the result? Only contemptuous ridicule or polite indifference! May we not suppose that the apostle learned there, as he had never perhaps learned before, the truth which he afterwards so emphatically enunciated when he wrote to the Corinthians. "The natural man receiveth not the things of the spirit of God, for they are foolishness to him; neither can he know them because they are spiritually discerned."[1] Perhaps also from this signal experiment the apostle learned that it is not by scientific disputation, not by logically confuting the errors which speculation or tradition may have instilled into men's minds, that the preachers of Christianity are to advance her cause; but rather by the simple, authoritative proclamation of those truths which constitute the substance of her religion, and the peculiar boon which she has to confer. If, scholar and thinker as he was, he had hitherto had some natural confidence in the power of intellect to force a path through men's minds for the truth, his experience at Athens, we may well believe, would go very far to disabuse him of all such notions. May not this experience thus have had a powerful

[1] 1 Cor. ii. 14.

effect in the discipline of the apostle's own mind, and contributed materially to his future success as a herald of the cross? May it not have been needful for him to learn in this pungent way that the preaching of the cross is foolishness to men, in order that all the more he might have faith in it as the wisdom of God? Certain it is, that when he passed from Athens to Corinth, it was with a resolution to renounce all attempts to secure his end by excellency of speech and of wisdom, and a firm determination to know nothing among men save Jesus Christ and Him crucified. The apostle was thus in reality a gainer by what seemed only a waste of time and strength, and a permanent advantage was secured for the Christian cause from what seemed at first an ignominious defeat.

But the apostle's labours were not wholly in vain, even with respect to the end he had directly in view. Whilst the majority turned away from his message, there were some who "clave to him and believed." Special mention is made of two of these,

Dionysius the Areopagite, that is, one of the judges in the court of the Areopagus, and a female, probably a person of some note in the city, named Damaris. Of these we know nothing further with any certainty. Eusebius, the church historian, says that Dionysius was the first bishop of the Christian Church in Athens,[1] which is by no means improbable; and a later tradition represents him as having died the death of a martyr for the truth.[2] A few besides these two embraced the Apostle's doctrines, and this handful constituted the germ of the Church at Athens, a church which continued for centuries, and was not without rendering important services to the Christian cause.

From the association of heathenism with the art and philosophy of Athens, it retained its hold upon the public mind more extensively and for a longer period in that city than in other places where Christianity had been planted, and in consequence of this the

---

[1] *Hist. Eccl.* iii. 4; iv. 23.
[2] Nicephorus, *Hist. Eccl.* iii. 11.

Church at Athens never rose to that place of prominence which some churches in other and far less important cities of Greece attained. From it, however, came forth the first Christian apologists after the days of the apostles, Quadratus and Aristides, who wrote in the time of the emperor Hadrian,[1] in the early part of the second century. Their apologies have not been preserved, but in them we have to recognise the earliest attempts at a systematic arrangement of the truths of revelation, and in them also there is reason to believe that for the first time the attempt was made to combine Hellenic speculation with Christianity—a tendency which was destined, for good or for evil, to exercise a potent influence on the form of Christian thought in all subsequent time. Athens may thus be regarded as the cradle of systematic theology, and the birth-place of Christian philosophy. In her schools also some of the great theologians of the early

---

[1] Euseb. *Hist. Eccl.* iv. 3 ; Hieron. *Catal. Scriptor. Eccles.* 19, 20, *Opera* i. p. 274.

Eastern Church—Clement of Alexandria, Basil the Great, and Gregory of Nazianzum, received their scientific training; and it was from the Church at Athens that the writings came forth which are known under the name of Dionysius the Areopagite, though certainly not written by him, and which exercised a mighty influence on the speculative and religious life of the Middle Ages. Not in vain, therefore, had St. Paul disputed in the Agora, and discoursed on Mars' Hill, at Athens; though he had to go away mortified and apparently defeated, he had, nevertheless, sown a seed which bore fruit for centuries afterwards, and the influence of which has outlived that of the philosophers by whom the apostle was despised and ridiculed.

XI.

St. Paul's abiding confidence in Christianity as the Power of God and the Wisdom of God.

How long the apostle remained in Athens after delivering his discourse on Mars' Hill cannot be accurately ascertained. From the fact that Timothy joined him there, and was again despatched by him to Macedonia, previous to rejoining him at Corinth, it may be presumed that he did not quit Athens immediately after that occurrence.[1] It is evident, also, that he was not compelled to leave it by any violence, but departed from it at his own convenience;[2] which is also in favour of that supposition. Assuming this,

[1] 1 Thes. iii. 1 ; comp. Paley, *Horæ Paulinæ*, ch. ix., No. 4.   [2] Acts xviii. 1.

we may suppose that St. Paul would be occupied in carrying forward the work he had begun by expounding to the new converts "the way of the Lord more perfectly," receiving the visits of inquirers and sincere doubters, arranging for the orderly conducting of Christian worship, and the polity of the church in the infant society of which he had laid the foundation, and exhorting the brethren "that with purpose of heart they should cleave unto the Lord."[1] But he does not appear to have again addressed any public assembly there. His oration on Mars' Hill was his first and last attempt to press his doctrines on the attention of the "Men of Athens."

The apostle could hardly fail to feel that in this his first great encounter with the culture and philosophy of the West he had been foiled as respects the main end of his mission. But whilst, as already hinted, this experience may have been of advantage to him in leading him to adopt methods

[1] Acts xi. 23.

of presenting his doctrine better adapted to carry conviction to the hearts of those he addressed; it did not for a moment shake his conviction of the truth of the message which he carried, or of its fitness to promote the great ends which it contemplated in the salvation of mankind. On the contrary, his defeat, if so it must be called, only made him cleave the more ardently to the doctrines he had to teach, and to glory more confidently in their inherent power, independent of the aid of human rhetoric, argument, or science. He had had painful experience that the doctrine of Christ and Him crucified was "to the Jews a stumbling-block and to the Greeks foolishness." The former denounced it as "weakness," because it had not been introduced with such startling manifestations of the divine power as those which had accompanied the establishment of the Mosaic economy; the latter derided it as "foolishness," because it did not present a system of doctrine addressed to the speculative reason. But the apostle knew that the real obstacle in both cases arose from the blindness and obduracy of their hearts, which would not suffer them to look at it fairly, to judge of it candidly, or to yield it the belief which it demanded and deserved. In itself, and in the experience of all whose hearts God had opened by His divine call to attend to it and receive it, the apostle knew that it was "the power of God and the wisdom of God."[1] And, therefore, his deliberate and final resolution was to go on preaching the gospel of Christ, assured that it was " the power of God unto salvation to every one that believed it."[2]

These assertions of the apostle bring before our consideration the position that Christianity, viewed as a proclamation of "Christ and Him crucified,"—that is, of salvation for guilty men through an atonement wrought out by Jesus Christ as incarnate God, and consummated by His death upon the cross,—is in all respects adapted to secure the end it has in view, the salvation of men's souls; and so is, experimentally and in its effects,

[1] 1 Cor. i. 23, 24.   [2] Rom. i. 16.

a manifestation of the power and wisdom of God.

The *wisdom* of any plan or scheme, as tested by its effects, is evinced by the excellency of these effects on the one hand, and the simplicity and fitness of the means by which they are produced upon the other. If the things it accomplishes be not in themselves of importance, we are apt to conclude that, whatever of effort has been expended in the production of them is only so much energy thrown away; and if the means by which results, however important, are achieved, be cumbrous, complicated, and difficult to set in operation, we cannot regard them as indicating large resources or great skill on the part of the contriver. It is when excellence of end is combined with simplicity and suitableness of instrumentality that we willingly accord the praise of *wisdom* to the scheme.

Power, on the other hand, as exhibited in the working of a plan, is seen in the sure and easy overcoming of obstacles which lie in the way of success. If these obstacles be many and serious, and yet be readily and effectually surmounted; or if the success of the scheme be endangered by many and alarming risks, and these be steadily and surely warded off, so that the enterprise advances without serious impediment to its intended issue, we at once recognise the presence of consummate power and energy, in the direction and working of the project.

Applying these tests to the scheme of human redemption, by means of the atoning death of Christ, we shall see, limited though our power of comprehending such a subject in all its bearings may be, enough to satisfy us that in it we have a transcendent and unequalled manifestation of the power of God and the wisdom of God.

The field embraced under the head of the effects or working of the scheme of redemption is immensely wide: so wide that it is impossible for us to comprehend it even in thought. It reaches through all duration, and we may say through all extension; nay, it transcends the boundaries of time and space, for it stretches through eternity and reaches the throne of God Himself. There is no being whom it does not concern; no spot in creation where its influence does not penetrate; no point in the long lapse of duration at which its power has not been or will cease to be felt. By it the divine character is illustrated, the divine government vindicated, the divine law confirmed and magnified. By it holy angels are filled with new accessions of gladness, and lifted up to loftier heights of intelligence and wisdom. By it devils are taught how vain their craft, how impotent their devices, how feeble their resources when brought into collision with the divine beneficence and power. By it man is restored to his primeval dignity and more than his primeval felicity; and this world which Satan had seduced from its allegiance is brought back to its proper place in the kingdom of heaven. And through means of it all creation, sighing and groaning under burdens imposed on it by man's apostacy, anticipates a glorious deliverance, " waiting for the manifestation of the sons of God."[1] Over so vast a field no created eye can gaze. For us it " passeth knowledge." Ascend to what elevation we may, still the prospect stretches immeasurably away from us; and though at each ascending step our horizon widens and new scenes of grandeur and new forms of beauty come within our view; it is ever with the humbling yet gladdening consciousness that more, far more remains yet to be discerned; that scenes of brighter glory are yet to be unfolded, and forms of sweeter loveliness yet to be observed; and that the transcendent whole unfolds itself to no eye but that of Him of whose power and wisdom it is the living and crowning demonstration.

The part of this wide field which lies most before our view, and to which we shall at present confine ourselves, is the operation of the work of redemption, through Christ and Him crucified, upon the human race. And here there are two distinct aspects under which the

[1] Rom. viii. 19, ff.

subject may be viewed, the one of which has reference to the work of Christianity in the world at large, the other of which concerns the work of Christianity in each man's soul who is brought under its influence. It is only a cursory survey we can bestow upon either of these objects of contemplation.

I.

Glancing at the influence of Christianity upon the world at large, the first thing that challenges attention is *the exceeding excellence* of those results which Christianity has effected among men.

When the religion of Jesus Christ appeared in our world, the condition of mankind was, in a spiritual point of view, most deplorable. Among the Gentile nations all knowledge of the true God seemed to have fled from the minds of men. Whatever embers of divine truth still survived in any portion of the heathen world, were so covered over with the ashes of carnal passion and corruption that they burned with but a smouldering fervour, and yielded but a lurid glare. A splendid ceremonial, casting its flimsy veil over degrading superstitions, loathsome orgies, or cruel rites; a people sunk in vice, burdened by oppression, and blinded by ignorance; philosophy lending its aid to cast a denser shadow over the hopes of man; art contributing its resources to enervate and brutalise; all the bonds of society loosened as if it were about to resolve itself into its original elements:—these were the dark and broad lines that marked out the prevailing features of the heathen world at the dawn of Christianity. Nor was the state of things much better among the Jews, favoured though they were with the light of revelation; for that light was hid from them by the thick clouds of prejudice and ignorance which had gathered over their minds. A rigid adherence to forms; a proud pretension to the favour of God, that rested upon mere hereditary grounds; a haughty contempt for all other nations; an ingenuity in explaining scripture which had no other effect than to mislead, and give an apparent sanction from the Word of God to the vain fancies of their teachers; an utter abandonment of all the elements of true vital godliness; and a rampant hypocrisy and sensuality:—these were the features in Jewish society which formed the sad counterpart to those which cast so dark a colouring over the Gentile nations. It seemed the midnight of the world—a midnight without a moon, and with scarce the twinkling of a star. All was dark and cheerless; or if here and there a bright ray burst forth, it was but to struggle for a season with the invidious gloom, and then to disappear, leaving the darkness deeper than before.

It was when this darkness was at its worst that the Sun of Righteousness arose, and commenced a day which no night shall ever terminate. Filling at first but a narrow horizon, the light of this unsetting luminary gradually has spread until it embraces now portions of both hemispheres, and promises ere long to encircle the globe. Ere it had been many years at work Christianity proved its divinity by the mighty results it achieved. Before it ancient superstitions yielded up their sway; and the stiff formalisms of a shadowy economy gave place to living spiritual realities; and the spirit of man, disenchanted and emancipated, shook off its fetters and purged the filmy darkness from its eyes; and old traditions grew decrepid and wasted on their thrones; and religion came back to be a dweller in man's heart; and devotion lifted herself from the dust and put on the garment of holiness; and the reign of vice and sensuality became smitten as with a dead palsy; and the bonds of society were re-knit and made firmer than ever; and the fountains of loving-kindness were opened afresh, and made to pour their sweet waters where all before was bitterness and poison; and philosophy, instead of pandering to man's passions, became the minister of his virtues; and poetry dipped her sparkling cup in the river of the water of life; and art bathed herself in the light of

SIMPLICITY OF MEANS.

heaven; so that over the whole field of human interests, and pursuits, and aspirations, there at length spread an influence which, in the transcendent excellence of its effects, proclaims the surpassing wisdom of Him by whom the whole had been purposed and performed.

But the wisdom of God is further apparent in the progress of Christianity from the *simplicity* of the means employed by Him for this purpose. These means are of a kind so simple, that they at first hardly attracted the notice of the world, and when at last they were looked at, the world mocked and scorned them. A few poor, illiterate, simple-minded men went forth to convert and renovate the race—to tell the world that their master was incarnate deity, that he had died for the world's sins, that he had risen again from the dead, and had gone up into heaven, and that through Him there was the free remission of all sin and an inheritance of eternal felicity to all who would come unto God through Him. This was all.

No pomp of state,—no glare of worldly power,—no resources of worldly learning,—no artifices of carnal rhetoric,—no "excellency of speech,"—no pandering to the evil tastes of the multitude,—no courting the favour or the assistance of the great or wise; nothing but the plain and earnest telling of a plain and touching story by plain and sincere men—nothing but this was employed to work out those mighty results which, in the days of the apostles, marked and dignified the course of Christianity in the world. Nothing could be more simple than this. And so, when the apostles delivered their message to the Jews they ridiculed them, and said, "these men are full of new wine:"[1] and when they carried it to the Greeks, these professed votaries of wisdom turned from it contemptuously and said, "it is foolishness." And yet from among these very Jews and Greeks there were not a few who bowed before the might of that message, and yielded to it the willing testimony that what at first

[1] Acts ii. 13.

seemed to them foolishness and weakness, was indeed the wisdom and the power of God.

For the simplicity of these means is not more real or even more apparent than their *suitableness and adaptation to the end in view.* Let it be borne in mind that the design of the apostles and their Great Master was not to establish Christianity in the world by *any* means which might promise success. This religion is of such a nature, that it is possible for it to be propagated and established outwardly by means which shall entirely destroy its intrinsic power and excellence. If fraud or force, for instance, be used on its behalf, an injury and not a benefit is conferred upon it—a loss and not a gain secured for it; for, being a religion of truth, it would be self-contradictory to suppose it capable of reaping advantage from the aid of falsehood; and being a religion of love, it would be no less so to suppose it capable of being aided by oppression or tyranny. Again, as the aim of Christianity is to regulate man's whole being by principles and motives of a purely spiritual character, it can only interfere with this to mix up its appeals with anything which addresses itself to man's carnal and earthly nature; for what is this but to propose to wean man from the world by feeding him with the world's nutriment? And in fine, as it is the great design of the gospel of Christ to erect in man's soul an undivided empire for God, it is necessary that in plying him with the invitations of the gospel nothing be allowed to come between him and God, but that he shall be made to feel that it is not on the ground of human reasoning, or eloquence, or science, but on the ground of God's word to him that his hopes of pardon and grace must rest. Such being the avowed design of Christianity, who does not see in the means employed by God for its propagation an agency most wisely adapted to attain this end and no other? Had the apostles come working no miracles, it is evident that the proof of their divine commission would have been defective: had they wrought miracles more frequently than they did, they might have pandered to a mere idle love of excitement on the part of the populace, and incurred the risk of attaching to them a multitude who were attracted by their power, but had no real love for their doctrine. Had they been men of splendid abilities, able to wield all the weapons of rhetoric, and skilled in all the ingenuities of philosophy, they might have rested so much upon these as to hide from the people the purely divine character of their doctrine and mission. Had they put themselves under the protection of earthly authority, or sought to advance their cause by the resources of human power, the empire which they would have succeeded in founding would not have rested simply on the basis of the inherent truthfulness and worth of the doctrine they taught, but would have owed something at least to the external force by which it was surrounded and sustained. In short, had the machinery been less simple, unworldly, and spiritual than it was, the real end which was to be attained would have been lost, and another and inferior end substituted in its place. And as the instrumentality employed was thus the best adapted to the end designed, and was, at the same time, the most simple and natural that could have been used, it is impossible not to acknowledge in the attainment of such mighty results by such means, a glorious manifestation of the wisdom of God.

Thus far the facts adduced illustrate the *wisdom* of God as displayed in the Christian scheme of redemption; we have only to glance at the *obstacles* in the face of which this success was attained, to see how, by the progress of the gospel, is illustrated the *power* of God with which that wisdom is associated. These obstacles were of a kind which might well have discouraged and driven back any but men who felt that they were sustained by omnipotence. When we think how hard it is to effect even a slight reform in some long established and corrupt system; how the mind cleaves to that which has the sanction of antiquity and the authority of law; how interest, and fashion, and prejudice, and even sometimes the better feelings of our nature rise up against any attempts to displace venerable errors, or to supplant time-honoured usages:—we may well admire the marvellous boldness of the disciples of Christ, who went forth to demand the overthrow of all the religions that then enjoyed the homage of the race, and to claim undivided reverence for that of which they were the heralds. And when we consider the fewness of their numbers, the illiteracy and poverty in which the greater part of them had grown up, and the insignificance of the locality whence they emerged; when we glance at the singularly unpretending character of the machinery they employed, and the utter repulsiveness to human pride of the doctrines they proclaimed; when we see all the learning, and all the wealth, and all the power of the world bristling, with angry front, to forbid their progress and crush their enterprise; when we see kings unsheathing the sword, or kindling the fires of persecution; magistrates casting into prison and loading with chains; fierce mobs rushing to the hasty decision of stoning on the spot, or casting to the lions in the amphitheatre; and when we see how to meet all this the emissaries of the cross had no weapons but words, no resources but those of a simple story which philosophy heard with scorn, and which wit mocked and ridiculed, we may well stand in wonder at the courage which, in the face of such terrible odds, led the apostles of Christ to descend into the arena to do battle in His cause. No wonder that prudent men of the world thought these men beside themselves. But it was not so. These were no madmen, but right sober and prudent as well as earnest men. They knew perfectly what they were about—what they meant to do, and how they meant to do it. They were fully conscious of their own utter insufficiency, as of themselves, for so great an enterprise.

They felt themselves to be but fragile instruments—mere earthen vessels, ready to be broken into sherds at the first shock of the adversary. And yet they calmly contemplated the mighty work that was before them; and, without one faltering emotion, set themselves to do it. Whence this unexampled boldness? this more than Roman fortitude? Was it not from the firm assurance that the truth they announced is the power of God unto salvation? They knew that however humble the instrument, he becomes irresistible when the agent is the Almighty. They were assured that God had " chosen the foolish of the world to confound the wise, and the weak things of the world to confound the mighty, and base things of the world and things which are despised hath God chosen, yea, and things that are not to bring to nought things that are;"[1] and knowing this they gloried in their infirmity, and thought nothing too great for them to attempt and to do in their Master's cause. And as

[1] 1 Cor. i. 27, 28.

the good work advanced, as triumph after triumph was gained, as the altars of superstition began to fall, and the temples of idolatry to be closed, and men were seen hastening from all parts in obedience to the divine call, they pointed their admiring converts upward to the great source of all, and said, "We preach Christ and Him crucified—the *power of God.*"

The evidences thus afforded, by the operation of the scheme of redemption in the world, of the divine wisdom and power therein concentrated, have not been confined to the days of the apostles. In all succeeding ages the same evidences have been afforded wherever the gospel has been published, and in proportion to the freedom and purity with which it has been proclaimed. In our own day these evidences have been augmented with astonishing rapidity and to an overwhelming extent. By the labours of faithful men the gospel has been carried to nearly all the nations of the earth, and everywhere with the same results. In ancient cities, and in lonely wastes; over vast continents, and in the islands of distant seas; among nations of the highest culture, and tribes in the lowest grades of savagism; in the face of the most advanced science, and in spite of the densest ignorance; beside solemn temples, rich with the votive offerings of many generations, and around the frost palaces of new and noisy speculation:—everywhere, and with all kinds and classes of men the power of the gospel of Christ has made itself felt. It would be refusing to learn one of the great lessons of the world's history were we to turn aside from the evidence thus afforded, that the doctrine of Christ and Him crucified is the power of God and the wisdom of God.

II.

Let us now turn for a little to the other aspect under which the theme before us may be viewed, viz., that presented by the case of individuals who are brought under the influence of Christianity. Here, as under the other aspect, it is only in brief outline that we propose to consider the subject.

Look then for a moment at the mighty results to an individual of believing the apostolic doctrines. Here is a man who was once afar from God—resting under his righteous displeasure—awaiting the infliction of that terrible sentence which God has denounced against the workers of iniquity—having no hope of escape, and indifferent, perhaps, about futurity—with his heart full of worldliness, and it may be vice and pollution—hastening, as fast as time could carry him, to the judgment-seat of God, with all his guilt cleaving to him, and adding at every step to the tremendous load. Behold him now! He has been brought nigh to God; he has found the pardon of all his sin; he has been turned from the world, and has found a treasure which the world cannot give and cannot take away—a peace which passeth all understanding; he is filled with a joy unspeakable, and full of glory; his mind dwells on futurity, and borrows thence support under the trials, and stimulus to the duties of life; a spirit of holy fervour has been breathed into him, which carries him along an ever-ascending pathway of purity and love—a path that, as the shining light, shineth more and more unto the perfect day; and he waits but the summons of the Judge to enter his presence, with a good hope of a triumphant acquittal at his bar. How transcendent the change in that man's condition, and character, and prospects! And how simply has it all been brought about—by the mere reception and realisation of the truth concerning Christ and Him crucified! And in spite of what tremendous obstacles has this been achieved—obstacles arising from within and from without—obstacles from old habits of evil, alienation of heart from God, and the strong tide of custom and fashion—obstacles from the claims of worldly interest or reputation, and the incessant assaults of that practised deceiver who goeth about seeking whom he may deceive and destroy! Who can account for such things upon natural principles? Who can refuse to see in them a supernatural agency? Who can be so blind as not to perceive that in every such instance there is a trophy to the Divine grace, and a proof that the preaching of the cross, the doctrine of Christ, and Him crucified, is the power of God and the wisdom of God?

In judging of this subject, we should not forget that the redemption of the sinner is something more than a mere restoration to man's primeval state. It *is* this, but it is far more than this. It is the raising of him to a higher state of being and of blessedness than that from which Adam fell. By the work of the gospel on his soul, man is taught more of God than he ever otherwise could have learned; he is brought nearer to God; he is placed under higher motives than ever to love and serve God; and he draws from the Divine favour restored a depth of joy which those who have never lost that favour cannot reach. How wonderful is this! What a work of power and wisdom is it thus to make man's misery the source to him of a higher bliss; to make his sin end in greater holiness and purity; and to cause a rebellion which threatened confusion to the empire of God, an occasion for establishing that empire more firmly than ever in the affections of all its happy subjects! Who can refuse to behold here the working of Him whose attribute it is "from seeming evil" to be "still educing good"—of Him who is "excellent in counsel" as well as "wonderful in working?"

Suppose that that planet which recently came within the cognizance of astronomers, were suddenly to be loosened from the bond which attaches it to the centre of our system, and to yield solely to that original impulse which sent it spinning through space, with what a maddening plunge would it burst away on its lawless career, and what fearful devastation might it not commit as it rushed through the peopled territories of the sidereal uni verse, and bounded impetuously on to the regions of eternal night! But suppose ere it had reached "the flaming bounds of space" an unseen power suddenly arrested it in its wild career, and stayed its furious and disastrous course, and once more poised it on its axis, and caused it to retrace its steps, and restored to it its lost attraction, and sent it again circling in sunshine and serenity around its original centre; should we not say, Here is the doing of the Almighty, and the All-wise? But, if besides this, that wandering planet were brought nearer to the sun, and, instead of existing in the far-off distance, were carried in from its chilling and cheerless remoteness, and placed first in brightness, and first in fertility, and first in glory among its sister spheres, would there be one of its inhabitants who would fail to see how their greatest calamity had been turned into their greatest blessing? and how that which threatened them with the extremity of evil had become the occasion of raising them to an unhoped-for eminence of bliss? And just so is it with that wandering race that has been rescued from destruction by the grace of God. It, too, had broken away from the power that bound it to the moral centre of the universe, and had plunged far and fearfully into the abyss of moral darkness, and was hastening with disastrous speed to the verge of eternal ruin. But its downward career has been stopped; and it has been brought back to the regions of light and peace; and it feels again the power that bids it circle around the centre of its being. Nor is this all. Now that it has been brought back, it comes under the influence of a new and a nobler law; in consequence of which, at each revolution, the sphere of its orbit contracts, and it draws nearer and nearer to the centre, until at length having passed within the innermost circle of created being, it shall roll first in place among the sons of light, an eternal monument of the wisdom and the power of God.

And from what point shall we—you and I, reader—behold this grand apotheosis of our race? Shall it be from the midst of the glorified and exulting band itself, or from some other point in the universe of God? Shall we form part of those whose glory, surpassing that of seraphim, shall eternally reflect the immediate light of God, and who

> "Nearest the throne, and first in song,
> Their hallelujahs loud shall raise;
> While wondering angels round them throng,
> And swell the chorus of their praise?"

Or must all this glory and joy, shared by beings of our own race, be viewed by us as something in which we have and can have no share? Alas for those of our race of whom, though they have heard the gospel preached, this latter shall be the sad, the eternal destiny! From afar—on the other side of an impassable gulf—"being in torment"—suffering the terrible agony of a bitter and hopeless remorse—lost, for ever lost—they shall behold the unutterable joy, the immeasurable glory of the redeemed before the throne; and the sight will add to their pangs, not the gnawings of envy but the keen and poison pointed stings of self-reproach. For wherefore are *they* excluded from that happy band? Why this difference between them and beings of the same race and nature and nurture with themselves? Conscience supplies the reason. It tells of sin indulged, of guilt retained, of warnings neglected, of truth despised, of God insulted, of justice dared, of mercy scorned —a fearful tale, not to be gainsaid, never to be forgotten! Would *you* have conscience tell this tale to you all through eternity? There is but one way with certainty to avoid this. Accept now the doctrine in which the apostle gloried. Take Christ crucified as your Saviour; rest on the merit of His atoning death: confide in Him as able and willing to save to the uttermost all that come unto God through Him; and through Him you shall find acceptance with God, be placed among

His children, and in the great day of the Lord shall lift up your heads with joy as those for whom the Saviour has secured an inheritance in light.

THE END.

Printed by R. & R. CLARK, *Edinburgh.*

www.ingramcontent.com/pod-product-compliance
Lightning Source LLC
Chambersburg PA
CBHW021204230426
43667CB00006B/549